IDEAL HOME
BOOK OF
HOME
IMPROVEMENTS

IDEAL HOME
BOOK OF
HOME
IMPROVEMENTS

Consultant Editor: Ned Halley

Hamlyn

London · New York · Sydney · Toronto

Ideal Home Book of Home Improvements is based largely
on a series of articles published in *Ideal Home* magazine.
Authors and illustrators whose original work is included
in this volume are as follows: Brian Aldred, Dick Barnard, Lynn
Barnett, Jim Colthorpe, Linda Gray, Ned Halley, Don
Kidman, John Love, John Sanders, Tony Simmonds, Judy
Smith, George Wallace-Clark

The publishers gratefully acknowledge the cooperation
and assistance offered by the editor of *Ideal Home*.
Terence Whelan, in preparing this book.

Front cover photography, James Jackson

First published in 1984 by
The Hamlyn Publishing Group Limited
London · New York · Sydney· Toronto
Astronaut House, Feltham, Middlesex, England

ISBN 0 600 34732 X

Printed in Spain

CONTENTS

INTRODUCTION

Do you know what's going on under your own roof? To keep up your home's appearance, comfort and good state of repair, it is invaluable to have some knowledge of how the whole place works – from what the walls and floors are made of to where the pipes and wires run, from which tap to turn to shut off the water main to why doors tend to stick.

Even if your interest in doing your own home improving extends only as far as decorating or putting up the odd shelf, understanding your home is still crucial. After all, if you have no idea what your walls are made of, or how thick they are, do you dare to even attempt to knock a nail into one of them?

This book is largely devoted, there-fore, to explaining in plain language just how each part of the home is put together, what can go wrong and what you can do – or pay someone else to do – to put it right.

This comprehensive reference book guides you through the techniques and materials used to build the homes most of us occupy today – from period gem to ultra-modern house. Every important

aspect of the structure is covered: floors and ceilings, windows and doors, lighting and plumbing, heating and insulation.

But this is to describe only one part of its purpose because this is, above all, a book of ideas – ideas for improving your home in all sorts of ways and for all kinds of reasons.

In every part of the home where there's room for improvement, you will find guidance in these pages. There are ideas on decorating, equipping and

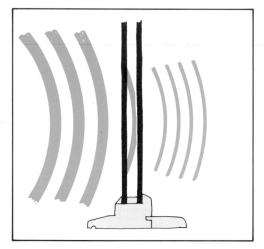

furnishing, heating, lighting and making structural changes to each room. Kitchen, bathroom, living room, dining room – all are covered in detail. And to inspire your decorator's eye, every section is illustrated by photographs full of ingenious and imaginative ideas.

This is not intended to be a do-it-yourself book. Each section includes projects that a reasonably handy person might well be able to undertake, but where the chapters describe work requiring special skills – for example, at roof level, or installing certain types of insulation – the text is quite clear that professionals should be called in.

In one respect, however, doing it yourself is certainly the best method – and that's when it comes to decorating. Today's decorative materials and tools are specifically manufactured for the convenience of DIY decorators, so most jobs are well within the average householder's scope.

A major section of the book is there-

fore concerned with all kinds of decorating work. Not just painting and papering, but tiling, putting up timber cladding and laying floorings, too. There is advice on the types of materials to use in different circumstances, and tips on colour scheming.

In the area of major improvements the book deals with that most radical improvement of all, the home extension. With the cost of moving house today now so high, more and more homeowners are deciding to add to the size of their existing homes rather than spend thousands of pounds on the numerous fees, commissions and taxes that are inevitably creamed off the home-mover's meagre budget.

A home extension is very much a personal thing, of course, built strictly according to individual needs. Coverage of this important topic, therefore, concentrates on that most bewildering aspect of extending: planning permission. The planning restrictions on everything from a new porch to a loft conversion or major extension are explained in detail – helping the reader form an idea of what sort of addition may be permissible for his or her particular home. Aided by illustrations, the sections dealing with adding on suggest numerous ideas for increasing the space in your home by way of conversion and extension – always bearing in mind the limits imposed under the planning laws.

The final chapters cover those areas outside the house that are so often in need of improvement – the paving, plus garden hedges, fences and walls. There's advice, too, on making improvements to your garage, or adding one.

Improving your home in the many ways covered in this book makes a lot of sense. It adds to its value, it increases the pleasure you get from living there – and actually doing the work can be a very pleasing and rewarding activity in itself.

If this book helps you to understand your home better, and the many fascinating things that you can do to make more of it, then its purpose will have been amply fulfilled.

1.
HOW IS YOUR HOME BUILT?

To plan any improvement project, from putting up shelves to adding an extension, you need to know by what method your home has been constructed. Walls, floors and roof may be of several different types – and you can usually tell which, according to when your house was built.

Before the railways made long-distance transport of materials an economic proposition, methods of building were largely dictated by the local availability of stone, timber and other vital commodities.

Homes built in the Georgian period (1714 to 1830) or earlier therefore tend to be radically varied in the style and quality of their construction. This is a point of architectural history well worth bearing in mind if you are considering buying any home with 'period charm'. Be sure first to have it structurally surveyed by a qualified, local expert.

For most of us, of course, home is unlikely to be much more than a century old, and thus built along much more standardized lines. With the spread of the railway networks in the nineteenth

Opposite, below, from left Surviving Georgian houses are mostly very elegant, but the quality of construction varies. A surveyor's advice is indispensable before buying or improving. A more dependable proposition is the craftsman-built and substantial Victorian town house (*centre*) or, more modestly, the deceptively spacious terraced home of the same period (*right*).

Below, from left Basic between-the-wars semi-detached features bay windows with half-timbering and pebbledashed, low-cost walls. Typical 'spec-builder' house (*centre*) of around 1934 has curved windows, but standard construction. Concrete canopy and glazed pantiles denote the period. Today's 'spec' house (*right*) uses plastic for pipes, cladding, and even for windows.

century, universal materials – such as Welsh slate for roofing – soon began country-wide styles of housing, with relatively minor local variations.

The Victorian town house

Spacious and formal in layout, the large Victorian houses built in stately boulevards for the prosperous middle classes had rooms of a size unknown in today's homes. Brick-built throughout, often with party walls as much as 46cm (18in) thick, these splendid buildings had 'engineered' roofing timberwork, allowing wider spans. Glass was becoming available in wider spans, so windows were generous in size.

Most of the great three- and four-storey houses have long since been converted to flats, but the more modest terraced homes of the era, built to the impeccable standards of Victorian craftsmanship, still stand in their thousands today.

Between the wars

The 1920s brought the ubiquitous semi-detached house, with bay windows and low-cost 'brick-bat' walls. Style was very often 'Mock Tudor'. This period also brought the reinforced concrete house in 'Odeon' style, with cantilevered floors to allow unbroken expanses of window, some even curved.

Cantilevered construction represented a complete break from traditional building techniques, but the style that succeeded it, in the 1930s, the 'modern, spec-builder' house, reverted to Victorian principles, adopting a few more recent refinements, such as curved steel windows, cavity walls and metal mesh rather than laths as a plaster base.

Up to today

Immediately after the last war, large numbers of 'chalet-type' houses were built. With a huge roof and minimal brickwork, it was a cheap construction technique. Dormer windows and sloping ceilings made upstairs rooms attractive, if chilly. Downstairs were cavity walls and timber or concrete floors.

Today, cavity-wall construction remains the dominant method, with outer skins of brick and inner walls of building blocks with uprated insulation value. Roofing tiles are replacing slate, and plastic is widely in use for guttering, tanks and elsewhere. Timber, on the other hand, is used sparingly: fat, heavy beams have given way to slim timbers designed to take the same weight.

Victorian Terrace House

The typical plan for the modest Victorian terrace consists of two main rooms per floor with a rear extension (usually the kitchen with a bedroom above). In two- or three-storey houses this arrangement gives the maximum space with relatively little frontage.

While many of these terraces were built to a high standard, there are nevertheless some common weaknesses. For example, thin dividing walls – as little as 11 cm (4½in) – can mean poor sound insulation; damp-proof courses are rare, and many terraces have no oversite concrete, so there is bare earth under the floorboards.

Larger Victorian houses do have very much thicker party walls, and many have spacious basements. Most Victorian basements rely on thickness of walls to keep out water, often using a hard industrial brick. This is not always successful, so it may be necessary to 'tank' a damp basement before using it. This involves lining the walls with bitumen or (asphalt), fixing Newtonite corrugated boarding, then plastering over. The corrugations allow the walls to 'breathe'. The floor needs a damp-proof course, screeding and finish.

Another potential problem may be the windows, which are usually sashes. They are difficult to draught-proof, and tend to rot, particularly where the woodwork meets the sill. Beadings also suffer regularly from rot, and broken sash cords are not uncommon – a laborious task to replace.

Complete replacement windows should be chosen with the greatest care for style, in order to avoid clashes with the house's original style.

Main picture The structure of a typical, small Victorian terrace house. Slate or tile roof over 'engineered' timbers is often in need of improvement: old mortar and lead flashing at roof joints can mean leaks, or slates themselves may need replacing. On external walls, pointing may need renewing, so that it throws off water – especially from walls only one brick thick – and prevents damp penetrating. Internal walls are commonly lath and plaster on timber studs, so fixtures such as shelving must be secured to the timbers as laths are notoriously weak. Load-bearing internal walls are brick. Lack of a damp proof course is common. Floor joists at ground level rest on brick supporting walls: water soaks up from the ground and into the timber. Solid floors with quarry tiles can let moisture seep through the adjoining walls,

ruining the timbers. On the first floor, the joists usually rest on a timber wall plate; if this wood shrinks (and, being set into an external wall, it often does), the joists may settle. The bricks above may consequently lean inwards a little and the walls can take on a bowed appearance.

Right, from top Roofing: Slates or tiles are fixed to battens over rafters. Slates are nailed every course, tiles usually one in five. Ceilings: laths nailed to floor joists, a coat of lime mortar and a finishing coat. Stairs: wedges securing treads and risers shrink to cause creaking – hammer back to cure.

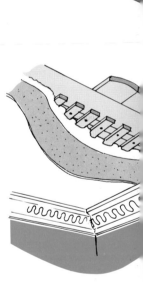

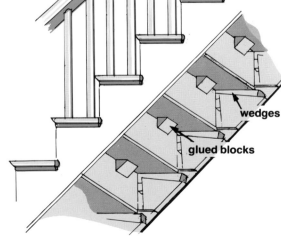

wedges

glued blocks

dormer wi

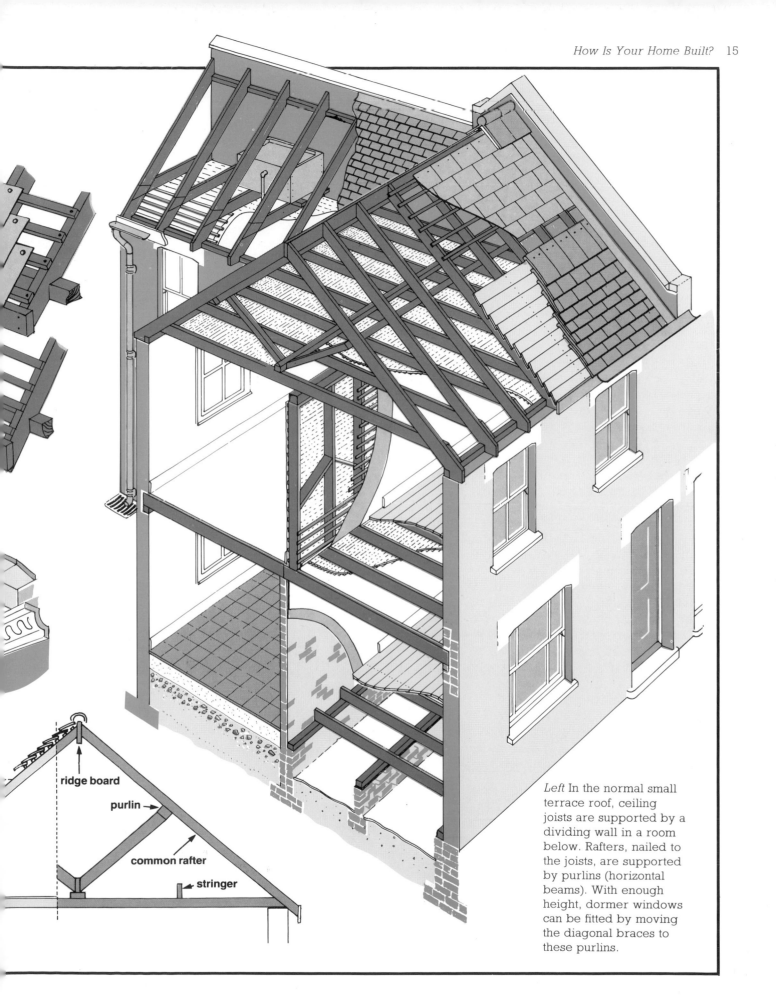

ridge board

purlin

common rafter

stringer

Left In the normal small terrace roof, ceiling joists are supported by a dividing wall in a room below. Rafters, nailed to the joists, are supported by purlins (horizontal beams). With enough height, dormer windows can be fitted by moving the diagonal braces to these purlins.

The 'Mock Tudor' House

Main picture Typically, two reception rooms and kitchen on ground floor; three bedrooms and bathroom above. Chimney stacks usually back-to-back in semis. Exterior walls 32cm (13in) solid brick on ground floor and 22cm (9in) above in earlier houses. Later ones have 28cm (11in) cavity walls. Partition walls are brick or, latterly, breeze block or stud/plaster. Shallow foundations can cause cracks at the base of the bay. Sills, mostly oak, may rot from below. Main window frames support the floor above.

Above right Many of these houses have high roofs (constructed Victorian-style) suitable for loft rooms. In better houses, the roofs are made by fixing the thick edge of the weatherboard so that it serves as a ridge for the tile nibs.

Right Oak-strip floors were popular in better-built houses, either laid on battens set in concrete screed, or fixed over a sub-floor of tongued-and-grooved boards. Parquet was often set in a layer of tar on top of concrete.

The 'Spec Builder' House

Main picture With curved windows reminiscent of the earlier 'Odeon' style, this typical 1930s home also features a reinforced concrete canopy over the front door and porthole windows. But the main construction is still basically Victorian. Exterior walls are usually cavity with breeze-block inner walls. Extruded clay blocks were used for partition walls. With the new, hard plasters, they gave a good finish. Some houses had lath and plaster ceilings but many used metal mesh as a base for plasterwork.

'Through' living-rooms were supported in the centre by a rolled steel joist. Most of these houses have good damp proof courses but these were often rendered over – allowing moisture to rise in the rendering and bridging the damp proof course. The metal windows need regular painting and removal of rust. The smooth rendering also needs regular repainting as the surface does not throw off water like a roughcast or pebbledash finish.

Top, right Pantiles need a good roofing felt to keep out rain and draughts (rain can blow in under the laps). Standard roof construction has some of its weight over the bay taken on a pair of joists spanning the opening.

Today's House

Main picture Typically, rooms downstairs are large, including a spacious kitchen-cum-dining room and a 'through' living-room. Rolled steel joists are often used to support the timbers of the floor above where the open-plan layout is particularly wide. Inner skins of the cavity walls and the internal walls are made of building blocks – these give added insulation value. Upper floors are formed by thin, deep joists which need herringbone bracing to prevent them twisting and thus cracking the plasterboard ceiling below. Tongued and grooved chipboard panels 2.4m by 1.2m or 600mm (8ft by 4 or 2ft) replace floorboards. Downstairs, solid floors are usual, with a continuous damp proof course covered in 50mm (2in) screed, finished with thermoplastic tiles or a composition woodblock or parquet-type floor. Heating ducts and pipework are often incorporated into the main concrete. Wiring, now pvc-insulated, usually lies in grooves in walls and is plastered over. 'Wet' central heating systems use small-bore copper pipe with soldered fittings – now virtually a standard feature in new houses. Soil pipes above and below ground are formed in pvc and most of the waste pipes and overflow pipes are of the same type of material. Polythene or glass-fibre water cisterns replace

the old, rust-prone water tank. Plastic gutters and downpipes save both on painting and maintenance. They are trouble-free if properly fixed with sufficient brackets to avoid dips in the run.

Today, even windows may be plastic (upvc) – or aluminium or steel as well as wood. Casement and revolving windows are common, sashes rare.

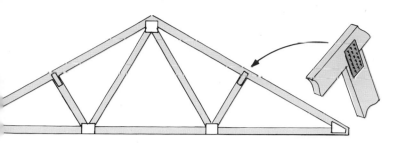

A typically economical way of using today's expensive timber is the roof truss. Very thin wood, which would have proved quite useless in previous roofing techniques, is joined by metal fixings to form a number of strongly built triangles that span wide areas. Roofing tiles are lighter, too.

The Timber-Frame House

About a quarter of all new houses built in Britain are based on the timber-frame principle. From the outside, timber-frame houses look much like any other type, being clad in fire-resistant materials such as brick or tile. Strict building regulations call for high standards of fire-proofing. According to the National Housebuilding Council, indeed, the overall required specifications for timber-frame houses are more demanding in this country than anywhere in the world.

One main advantage of this type of construction is the excellent insulation value produced by incorporating glass-fibre quilt into the inner wall. Wood itself is an incomparable insulator.

The timber inner wall, which is load-bearing, is often made up in sections and delivered complete to the construction site. The structure can therefore be erected speedily, and the outer skin built around the shell. Wall ties join the inner and outer walls.

The inner wall is lined with a polythene vapour barrier and plasterboard, which is nailed to the uprights and noggins (the horizontal timbers bracing the uprights). Over the other side of the timber frame is fixed a ply outer skin covered with building paper.

Before attempting to make any major alterations to a timber-frame house, you should seek expert advice, as the load-bearing wood structure cannot simply be breached for, say, a new doorway or an opening into an extension.

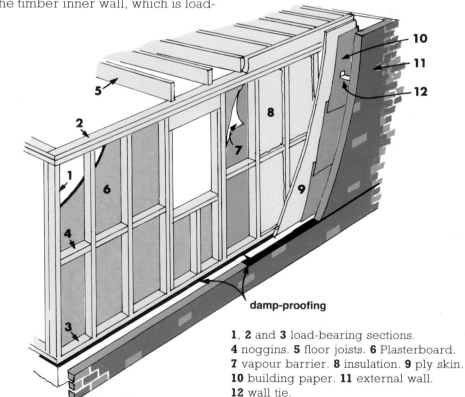

damp-proofing

1, 2 and 3 load-bearing sections.
4 noggins. 5 floor joists. 6 Plasterboard.
7 vapour barrier. 8 insulation. 9 ply skin.
10 building paper. 11 external wall.
12 wall tie.

2.
OUTWARD APPEARANCES

Keeping the outside of your house in good trim is a good deal more than a cosmetic exercise. Regular maintenance and repair can successfully prevent any really serious deterioration, and thus avert disasters such as a leaking roof, collapsing gutter or crumbling and falling masonry.

On the roof

Check the roof annually for faults. What you cannot see from inside the loft you can usually check from an upstairs room or from the outside, with the assistance of a pair of binoculars. Be on the lookout particularly for any gaps – or leaks – around valleys, vent pipes and chimneys where the flashing might be faulty. These sheets of lead or zinc, which fill the gaps which the slates or tiles cannot cover, can be renewed, or repaired with bitumen emulsion and bitumen-backed metal tape.

Loose slates or tiles represent another common problem. Making replacements is not really a difficult job, but finding matching tiles might well be. However, local roofing firms often keep a stock of second-hand tiles for this particular purpose.

If a large area of roof looks as if it is in need of attention a complete re-roofing may be the only solution, although some treatments – such as sealing the outer surface with resin or spraying the underside with polyurethane foam – can effect at least an acceptable temporary repair.

Re-roofing must be done by a competent contractor, and the new materials must not be too heavy for the old rafters. If in doubt, get advice from a qualified surveyor. As part of a roof replacement job, do consider felting: it improves weatherproofing and insulation considerably.

Chimney check

While the roof is under repair, have the chimney stack inspected. Loose chimney pots are dangerous. If the chimney is no longer in use, have it capped – incorporating air holes to ventilate the flue. Check, too, for cracks and any signs that the stack is leaning. If it is, seek expert advice.

Gutters

Each autumn, clean out dead leaves and other debris, taking care not to scrape it into the downpipes.

Leaks are most commonly caused by poor joins between lengths of guttering, while overflows may mean the guttering has been incorrectly fixed. There should be enough support brackets to prevent sags, and they should be positioned to provide a gentle slope to the downpipes. If the soffit (the board covering the rafter ends) or fascia board (fixed to the house wall below the eaves) to which the guttering is attached is rotten it should be replaced.

Old, deteriorated cast-iron guttering can be replaced with a plastic system – a job most people can take on themselves.

Wall protection

Bare brickwork needs little maintenance, but if the mortar pointing between bricks has become crumbly, it should be raked out and renewed – a skilled job best carried out by an expert if required over a large wall area.

The best way to inspire your own exterior decorator's eye is to look at what the neighbours have done. Any number of decorative ideas can be yours if you keep your eyes open when walking or driving about. Make a note of any colour combinations that particularly appeal to you, and which you think would translate well to your own house. The effect may rely on bold-coloured masonry paint or on something as subtle as the treatment of the window frames. Don't forget finishing touches such as paths, steps and door furniture, or the softness and natural colour provided by plants and shrubs.

Exterior ideas for a small Victorian house

You can change the personality of any house by means of exterior decoration, as the four versions of a modest terrace home on this page demonstrate.

Top, left Victorian brickwork often takes on a pleasant patina that only age can give. So here the walls are simply coated with a clear silicone fluid to protect the ageing surface, and the stonework washed down and given a coat of white cement paint.

Top, right Here the brickwork has been repointed (for colour effects, repoint with material such as Blue Circle Colourmix). The stonework has been decorated with masonry paint. Window boxes and awnings, plus a bright-red door, produce a very cheerful aspect.

Below, left Here the house has been completely rendered and painted two-tone in brown and pink, with the stonework picked out in white. This visually decreases its narrowness and height.

Below, right Where traffic fumes are particularly bad, a dark scheme with white stonework looks fresh and, with occasional repainting of the white trim, will look good for years. Dark greens and blues are fine in seaside areas but tend to look wrong in the country where terracotta, dark brown or deep mustard shades seem to fit in more naturally.

Making an entrance

Your front door is very much the focal point of your home's exterior. It should say 'welcome' to all your visitors. Whether it's a traditional-style, solid wood door complete with brass trimmings, or a simple flush door painted in a strong, plain colour it should create a good impression. A front door which is in poor condition will let down the overall appearance of any house, however well decorated the rest of the exterior might be.

Internal doors, too, are important decorative features and should be considered in the context of the room's décor, adding to its style and perhaps playing a significant part in improving the lighting conditions.

External doors

Does your front door need improvement? If it looks dilapidated, or it sticks or lets in draughts, or the lock seems less than secure, you should give priority to putting it right – and not just for appearances' sake.

Painting Perhaps all it needs is a coat of paint. If the old paintwork is in reasonable condition, rub it down with medium or fine glasspaper. Apply undercoat and rub down again with glasspaper before putting on top coat.

Badly deteriorated paint should be stripped. Use a blowlamp, scraper and shave hook and work from the bottom up, starting with the mouldings. Keep the flame moving constantly to avoid scorching the wood.

If you prefer to use a chemical stripper (often preferable if the door consists largely of glass), apply it with a brush, leave for a few minutes and, when the paint blisters, scrape off carefully with a shave hook. Wash off all traces of stripper with warm water or white spirit (as per instructions on the container) and let the door dry completely.

Fill dents or holes with wood filler. You may notice that knots in the wood are exuding resin: scrape this off, rub over with glasspaper and apply two coats of knot sealer to the affected area.

Prime the clean, dry surface before painting with undercoat and gloss paint. Always rub down between coats to remove surface imperfections and ensure a smooth finish.

Varnishing Existing varnished surface must be carefully rubbed down with fine glasspaper, following the grain. Wipe over the surface with a damp cloth to clear all dust, then apply up to four coats of hard-wearing marine varnish. Ensure each coat is completely dry before applying the next.

Repairs If your front door sticks in winter but not in summer, the problem is probably humidity changes caused by the weather. But if it sticks year-round, it may be more serious. It may simply be due to too many layers of paint – in which case strip it down and repaint. But if it binds against the frame,

close it on to a sheet of carbon paper to determine the uneven areas and plane down the carbon-marked spots.

If the door binds on the hinge side, remove it, complete with hinges, pack the frame rebate with hardboard and rehang. If there is a gap on the hinge side, the hinges might not have been recessed enough to fit flush with the door and frame, in which case a deeper rebate should be cut into the frame. Alternatively, the screws may have worked themselves loose; pack the holes with a match or fibre plug.

Buying a new door If your front door is badly warped or rotten, you should replace it. You will find two types of door on offer at DIY shops and builders' merchants: flush and panel. Be sure to buy a door specifically made for exterior use. Before changing the door to a flat or maisonette consult the local council surveyor's office, as the door may have to comply with certain fire-resistance requirements.

Most front doors are of the panel type, made from solid wood components treated against rot. Softwood ones are meant to be painted, hardwoods varnished. Many styles incorporate glass panels which should be glazed with tempered safety glass.

Security A front door should be stout, secure and at least 45mm (1¾in) thick. A rim lock or nightlatch should be supplemented by a five- or six-lever mortise deadlock. Alternatively, fit a rim lock and a lockable handle which incorporates a deadlock.

Pay attention to security at the back door, too. It should be just as stout as the front door, and two security or mortise bolts at the top and bottom will give good protection. Remember, break-ins are as frequent through the back as they are through the front door.

Internal doors

You can buy softwood and hardwood types, either flush or panel. There are also louvre doors – popular as swinging, saloon-type doors or as bi-folds that are split and hinged down the centre so they can be folded into a limited space when opened.

Glass doors are a useful aid to lighten-

ing a room or hallway, but always use safety glass. In a door with a large pane, completely clear glass can be a hazard; in preference, choose smoked, patterned or frosted glass.

Decoration A natural timber door that has been painted can be stripped (either at home, with a proprietary chemical or by a professional firm). If the finish is not attractive, you can stain it before sealing and varnishing.

In many older properties, the original panelled doors may have been covered with a hardboard sheet to produce a flush finish. You can restore such doors by carefully removing the hardboard, filling the tack-holes with wood-filler, rubbing down (or stripping, if necessary) and decorating.

Below is a guide to the sequence of painting a door. Always paint the inner panels and moulds surrounding them first, then the cross members, finishing off with the uprights.

Remove door furniture to allow long brush strokes and keep the paint from running out of the corners of the mouldings, where it has a tendency to accumulate. Brush upwards away from the corners of mouldings to keep paint thin in these areas.

Finish the open edge of the door last in order to give you something to hold on to. Paint the hinge edge to match the outside of the door and the open edge to match the inside.

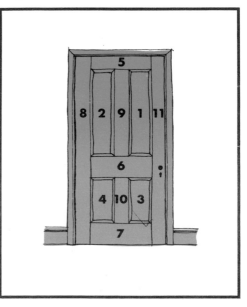

3.
A WARMER WELCOME

First impressions count for a lot, so giving a hallway a
welcoming look should be a priority. As well as adding to the
feeling of space by using appropriate floor and wall coverings,
you may be able to plan this usually limited area to make room
for some furnishings – which can make for a really stylish entry
to your home.

Left Traditional decor based on a dado rail. *Main picture* Stylish use of space at an open-plan entry.

Creating an attractive hallway involves practical as well as decorative considerations, because this is the part of the home that puts up with the worst punishment from passing traffic – from muddy boots to oversized prams, from ham-fisted delivery men to puddle-generating raincoats and umbrellas.

Floors, therefore, need special attention. Choose coverings that are hard-wearing, water-resistant and easy to clean. Vinyl tiles are the classic choice, but hard-wearing carpets such as berber or cord can be suitable, provided you are prepared to shampoo them at regular intervals. A carpet that matches the one laid on the stairs gives a pleasing continuity.

Many houses, particularly those of the Victorian and Edwardian periods, have stone-tiled hall floors which may have been hidden under lino or carpeting. These floors are often very handsome indeed as well as being practical. They can be cleaned up with patent chemicals available from builder's merchants. If your home has a tiled front step, the chances are the hallway will be similarly tiled.

Most period houses will have a dado rail running the length of hall and stairway walls at about waist height. By decorating the wall below this rail with a hard-wearing wall covering, you can minimize damage from prams, pushchairs and the like – leaving you free to decorate above with any material you choose. Note, however, that the half-and-half decorative effect produced in this way can make a hall look even longer and narrower than it does already.

To combat this decorative problem, use bright, cheerful colours for wall coverings – to boost the feeling of airy spaciousness. A large mirror on one wall can improve the sense of width, as can diagonal tiles laid on the floor. A mock ceiling arch at picture-rail height provides a convincing break in a long, narrow run of ceiling – again contributing to the look of width rather than length.

In a long and narrow hallway, two or three lights may be needed to avoid shadows. Wall lights are really only suitable in wider halls. Spotlights mounted on ceiling track are often ideal – and they can be used to illuminate pictures as well as lighting appropriate points in the hall such as the entrance, the coatrack and the foot of the stairs.

Open-plan houses, or those with large lobbies, present fewer decorative problems, even allowing space for a cloakroom or seating area or, as in the main picture on this page, a desk for letter-writing and telephoning. Many flats, of course, also offer ample lobby space of this sort.

Stairways

In most homes, the staircase itself is rarely singled out for treatment in its small shelf brackets fixed with short screws are a good substitute.

Minor squeaks can sometimes be cured from above by levering open the joint and 'lubricating' it with french chalk. Alternatively, squeeze in some woodworking glue and screw down through the tread into the top of the riser.

Worn or cracked tread nosings are another common problem. Here, you should chisel away the damage, cutting back to the middle of the riser's top edge, glue and screw a piece of scrap softwood in its place, then shape to match the original as closely as possible.

Finally, you may find a wall string has come adrift. In this case, refix using screws and wallplugs – trim ordinary plugs so you can push them into the masonry through the hole drilled in the string, or use plugs designed for refixing frames.

Decor ideas Choosing the decor is largely a matter of personal taste, but there are a few general points to bear in mind.

Remember that, in most homes, the stairwell counts as part of the entrance hall and landing, which means finding a scheme that suits all three. Since stairwells and landings are often gloomy, and since the hall needs to be welcoming, a light, bright colour scheme is probably best. Mirrors can help here, but be sure that reflections to not set up optical illusions that might confuse and endanger anyone using the stairs.

The practicalities of decorating the stairwell should also be taken into account. The height of the walls makes using steps and ladders difficult. And you should avoid very thin wall coverings, as long drops will tear easily and uneven stretching may make it hard to match up the pattern.

New flooring As part of the redecoration, new flooring could be fitted. You can simply treat the bare wood with a polyurethane seal if you wish but, because long-term tread wear is bound to lead to cracks and depressions in the surface, it is wiser to use some sort of covering such as vinyl or carpet.

Whichever covering you choose,

Staircase structure The various parts of the stairway (left) are known by some rather unfamiliar names. They are as follows: **1** Dado rail. **2** String. **3** Handrail. **4** Balustrade. **5** Nosing. **6** Newel post. **7** Tread. **8** Riser. **9** Bullnose step.

own right. Usually the hall and stairway are considered together when it comes to decoration, furnishing and improvements, and the full potential of the staircase is often lost in the general scheme. But the staircase is a major feature in any home, and deserves careful attention.

Basic repairs Squeaks are most commonly caused by loose joints, If you can get at the underside of the stairs, ensure that the wedges that help secure the treads and risers in the strings are tight by tapping their ends with a mallet. If any are missing, make replacements from scrap hardwood.

Make sure, too, that any blocks reinforcing the tread/riser joints are secure. These are only glued in place, so loose ones should be prised off, cleaned up and reglued. If blocks are missing, steel angle repair brackets or there are several points to remember. Most important is to ensure that the material is hard-wearing, because wear is localized and therefore severe.

Most good-quality vinyls should be suitable (check with your supplier). They should be stuck down all over and, ideally, protected with an additional, screw-on timber nosing.

Carpets should be of heavy domestic quality, and properly fitted, preferably according to the recommendations of the Technical Centre of the British Carpet Manufacturers Association, which are as follows:

The simple, open-tread stairway below is in complete decorative harmony with the style of this modern, open-plan living area.

Stair carpets, unless foam backed, should be laid with a good underlay in the form of runners or individual stair pads, with the pads overhanging each stair nosing. High-density (heavy-duty) foam-backed carpet may be used for stairs but special care should be taken when fixing. It is important the the lie of the pile is in the 'down-the-stairs' direction. An extra foot or so of carpet should be allowed so the length can be moved up or down at intervals to equalize wear. If possible, the position of the carpet should be altered twice in the first year of use. See that new staircases have well rounded, not sharp, nosings.

It is better to have a fitting that grips the carpet across its full width, rather than clips that hold the carpet only at its edges. Carpet which has a heavy-duty foam backing can be stuck down.

Carpets should be tacked at the top and bottom and held into the tread/riser angle with gripper strips. Alternatively, if you prefer, use stair-rods.

Make sure the flooring matches, or at least blends with, that in the hall and landing and that it looks right for the style of the stairs. In an older house, for example, carpet that is narrower than the treads (the remainder of the tread being painted) might be more in keeping than a fitted carpet. (It must, of course, be firmly fixed with gripper rods.)

Lighting Another simple way to improve a staircase is to upgrade the lighting. You not only make it look better, but also go a long way towards making it safe.

For safety, there are three basic rules. Illuminate the treads, in particular the nosings, as brightly as possible, leaving the risers in shadow. At the same time, because harsh contrasts can play tricks on the eye, you should arrange the main lights and their shades to soften the shadows with diffused light. Finally, avoid positioning any lights where they will shine in anyone's eyes.

Having found a suitable lighting scheme, think about switches. All lights needed for a stair or landing must be wired for two-way switching from the top and the bottom of the flight.

Above A decorative
scheme for a happy
landing.
Left An open tread
staircase means a more
spacious look.
Below Spirals are stylish
and practical.

Banisters and balustrades One radical
way of improving the look of a staircase
– and its safety – is to replace the
banisters and balustrades. This is a vital
job where the originals are at all
unstable.

There are many decoratively turned
spindles and handrails available 'off-
the-peg' from local do-it-yourself sup-
pliers and timber yards, and you can
buy complete kits specially made for
the purpose. As well as wooden materials, wrought iron panel balusters are
also available.

Given some modest skills and the
right tools, it should be possible to make
up a new balustrade yourself from
planed timber. Using a combination of
widths and sections, you can create an
interesting effect or you can cut the
timber into shapes with a jigsaw and

Right Traditional stairway with space-saving quarter landing.
Below A light and bright stairway is safe and attractive.
Bottom Many stairways offer unrivalled picture-hanging space.

template. You might even decide to do without a conventional balustrade and instead construct a safety barrier using, for example, parallel horizontal planks or plywood panels.

Whatever you choose, do make sure it blends in with the style of the existing stairs and with the decor as a whole. You should be able to find banisters and balustrades, even today, that will fit in with most period styles. Moreover, be careful to bear in mind that unusual balustrade designs may limit your decorating options should you wish to change the style of your hall and stairway at any time in the future.

5.
THE KITCHEN

In most households, the kitchen is the hub of activity; it's the one place families naturally congregate – to eat together, to play together or just to chat with the cook. So the kitchen should be a place that is not only practical to work in but a pleasure to be in, too.

The key to creating the kitchen that completely fits your needs, your preferences and your budget is careful planning. There are some useful guidelines you can follow when making your plans, but first you should consider some vital questions about your individual requirements:

1 How many people are there in the family and what are their ages? (A large household will need more equipment and storage room than one with no children, while a family with young children will have different equipment priorities from one with teenagers.)

2 How much cooking and food preparation do you do? How much entertaining do you do? (The amount of space you need and the planning for storage, preparation, cooking and serving relate to the amount of cooking you do and the equipment you require.)

3 Do you plan to eat in the kitchen? (If all meals are to be taken in the kitchen, you'll need to plan for a suitable dining area.)

4 Are you willing to consider structural alterations? (If your present kitchen is very small or has a large number of doors or windows, some structural work may facilitate a more efficient kitchen. Blocking up or moving a window or door could give you a better run of units and appliances. And a small kitchen could be enlarged by incorporating an adjacent larder, scullery or out-building.)

5 How much money do you want to spend? (This sum must cover any structural alterations which may be necessary, as well as units, appliances, fittings, flooring, plumbing, decorating and tiling.)

6 Do you wish to keep any existing appliances and units? (Immovable fixtures will have to be taken into account when you do your planning.)

tons, polythene bags, blanching baskets and so on.

As for non-freezer storage, you should have an adequate collection of shelves, hooks, deep-ventilated drawers, a couple of cupboards and perhaps a wine rack or two. (If you are a home-brewing enthusiast a utility room is ideal for working in and for storing both your equipment and your produce.) The storage space available can accommodate bulk-bought canned items, root vegetables, preserves and other food-stuffs not required in the kitchen on an everyday basis.

It may help to keep a record of exactly what you have in the freezer, where it is and how long it has been there – so consider putting up a notice board or blackboard for conveniently noting down the necessary details.

If your food storage area is set apart from the rest of the house it must have a substantial door fitted with a properly secure lock. Do not rely on a freezer lock alone.

If this room is to be used solely for vegetables and other food storage, fruit and preserves must be kept in the dark; so either cover or black the window and ensure that the artificial lighting is adequate. Fluorescent tubes would be the most suitable illumination.

Ventilation is particularly important, as the room should not be exposed to extremes of temperature or dramatic seasonal changes. The room should also be free from damp and it should have a level floor.

Overall design Having decided on the detailed uses to which you wish to put the room, the next step is overall design. Try to group all equipment for each type of function into a compact working area. Washing machines, for example, are best plumbed in under a work surface which, ideally, includes a sink, with storage space beneath. In a multi-purpose room, try to group food storage items such as the freezer, storage cupboard, food preparation work-top and so on in one area well away from the laundry area. (For 'module' schemes for utility rooms, see the illustrations on pages 64 and 65.)

Other items to consider for utility rooms as well as the functional equipment include a telephone extension – as a noisy washing machine in this isolated part of the house may make a distant ringing inaudible. Another good idea is to fit an extension door bell or an intercom linking the utility room to the rest of the house.

Safety If you have young children you may consider adding a small play area to the utility room so you can keep an eye on them while you work. A table, chairs, notice board for their pictures, cupboard for toys and so on could keep them safely occupied for at least as long as it takes you to do the laundry, prepare freezer food or get through the ironing.

Children, however, must not be able to touch any equipment, and you should make sure they cannot get into any trouble if you have to step out of the

Utility rooms can be put to many purposes, and there is no reason why they should not be decorative and pleasant to work in.

room for a moment. Ensure that power points have safety covers when not in use and that tools and cooking utensils are out of reach. Any chemicals, cleaning fluids, bleach, glue, paint solvent or other potentially harmful substances must always be safely locked away in a secure cupboard – a high shelf is not safe enough.

If you intend to use part of a bathroom as a utility area you *must* adhere to the legal safety regulations that apply to electricity.

First of all, it must be impossible for anyone to touch or turn on an electric appliance at the same time as a tap. In large bathrooms this simply means allowing enough distance between the two. In smaller rooms, you could consider concealing the appliance in a cupboard with the door hung so that when it's open it completely blocks the path to the taps.

Secondly, all your electrical appli-

ances must be fed from a fused connection unit, not from an ordinary socket.

Finally, all light fittings must be connected via a pull-cord system, not an ordinary switch, unless the switch is located outside the room.

Laundry equipment If you intend to stack a tumble dryer on top of a washing machine make sure the two are compatible and use appropriate stacking brackets. Check the overall dimensions to ensure that machines will fit the space available and that you have a gap of 50mm (2in) on each side of the appliances (unless they are built in) so they can be pulled out easily for maintenance. If space is limited and you do not plan to have a tumble dryer, consider buying a top-loading machine as these are narrower.

Flooring for a utility area should be hard-wearing, easy to clean and water-

There's no reason why a
bathroom should receive
less decorative attention
than any other room.
Planned with a bit of
flair, most bathrooms can
be pleasurable as well as
practical rooms

7.
THE BATHROOM

There is always wear and tear on the bathroom, so it tends to be the one room most urgently in need of improvement. Whether this simply involves renewing damp-damaged decor or a complete refit, careful planning is the key – to creating not just a practical scheme, but a bathroom which is a positive pleasure to be in.

The priorities

First decide on your present requirements and your future needs. Replanning a bathroom is a major project which should entail a long-term view, because your family's needs will undoubtedly change over the years.

Consider, therefore, the number of people in your family, and their ages. Do you have children, and are there likely to be any new additions to the family?

The type of fittings as well as their arrangement should be chosen to minimize congestion in the bathroom. If you have a bath and separate shower cubicle, for example, two people can wash simultaneously – a considerable convenience in households where everybody seems to want to use the bathroom at the same time.

Good lighting, convenient storage and a properly positioned and well-lit mirror are essentials not to be overlooked. You also need hooks and somewhere to put clothes down – ideally a comfortable chair if you can contrive space for it.

A towel rail, either heated or designed to fit over a radiator, is very valuable. You might consider putting laundry equipment, a boiler or immersion heater in the bathroom, but there are strict rules governing the installa-

tion of appliances using electricity in the bathroom (*see* page 75).

All these considerations have to be balanced against the space available, whether you are going to retain some existing fittings and how much you can afford to spend on new ones.

Size and location

If you are not satisfied with the size or shape of the existing bathroom or its location, you may be able to carry out some structural alterations. Remember to cost this into your overall budget.

Decide whether you want a separate WC, but remember that a small bathroom could be the consequence. Knocking down the partition wall between existing, separate bathroom and WC might, on the other hand, be sufficient to give you all the extra space you need.

Consider whether a separate WC, shower room or even a complete bathroom could be installed elsewhere in the house. Walk-in cupboards under stairs can sometimes be used, or you may be able to partition off part of a hall, landing or bedroom.

Bathrooms and shower rooms that are *en suite* can also be used as dressing rooms. If you haven't the space for a separate bathroom, consider the possibility of a vanitory unit or even a shower cubicle in the bedroom.

Space requirements

For your bathroom to be comfortable to use, you need certain minimum amounts of space around each fitting. In the Department of the Environment's Design Bulletin *Spaces in the home: Bathrooms and wcs* an optimum 'activity space' for each fitting is recommended. There will be a slight overlapping of some of the activity spaces in the well-planned bathroom, depending on the overall space, but try to ensure that the use of one fitting will not seriously impede that of another.

The drawings on the right illustrate the DoE's recommendations as follows:

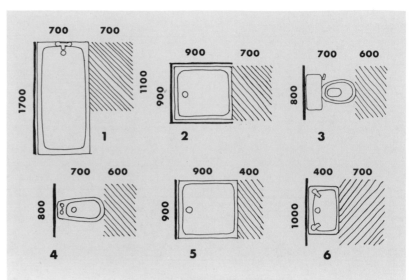

1. *Baths* need an activity space 1100mm long by 700mm wide, usually at the tap end of the bath. If there is a fixed shower screen at the tap end, the space will have to be at the other end.

2. and **5.** *Shower trays* enclosed on three sides need 700mm from the front or 400mm if the tray has only one side against a wall or is set into a corner.

3. *WCs* need 800mm by 600mm. The width should extend from 600mm in front of the bowl and there should be space on both sides right back to the cistern to allow comfortable use and plenty of room for cleaning.

4. *Bidets* need an activity area similar to that for WCs.

6. *Basins* require a large area of 700mm by 1000mm, or slightly less pro rata for a double basin.

Colour and style

Apart from white sanitary ware colours are divided into three price groups. The least expensive includes pastel pink (or coral), sky blue, primrose and turquoise. Next come the popular 'Sun

Making the most of space. *Above, left* An internal bathroom with mechanical ventilation. *Above, right* A bedroom washbasin concealed behind cupboard doors. *Opposite, above* A bath and basin built into a large bedroom, in matching style. *Opposite, below* A tall cupboard maximizes storage space in a narrow bathroom.

King', 'Pampas' and 'Avocado'. These two groups are standard, so there should be no variation of colour from one manufacturer to the other, although the shade may vary slightly according to the material that is used.

The third group consists of the most expensive fashion colours. These are not standard but, as a general rule, colours which have the same name will match, while those with different ones will not.

Popular group three colours include light shades such as 'Indian Ivory', 'Kashmir Beige' and 'Sandalwood'. Rich, deep colours are popular, too, but beware very obvious water marks if you live in a hard water area.

One recent development is the resurgence of patterned sanitary ware, which is now much more reasonably priced than it once was. Similarly, shaded sanitary ware (where colour graduates from the deepest to the lightest tone) is also reasonably priced.

Shapes have also been changing. The trend is towards larger, sculptured fittings with well-defined, almost geometric profiles.

Getting equipped

Baths have a standard size, roughly 1700mm by 700mm. Larger ones go up to about 1900mm long and 800mm wide, and shorter ones go down to about 1475mm long. Height from floor to rim is usually 500mm, but lower sides are available.

Oval, corner and round baths make exotic alternatives, but they take up more room – and more water.

Most common materials are vitreous-enamelled pressed steel, acrylic, glass-fibre-reinforced plastic (GRP) and porcelain-enamelled cast iron.

Pressed steel baths are inexpensive, reasonably long-lasting and available in many colours. Their coating is hard-wearing, but can chip. Continual use of abrasive cleaners will scratch and dull the surface.

Acrylic baths are lighter, economic and widely varied in shape and colour. Warm to the touch, they maintain water temperature well. Lighted cigarettes will burn acrylic – and avoid using abrasive cleaners. Even with steel frames, acrylic baths tend to be less rigid than steel ones. GRP has similar characteristics and is often used for more exotic baths.

Cast-iron baths are hard-wearing, rigid and keep their glossy surface for many years – but they are more expensive.

Although most baths have taps at the plug end they can be placed on the corner or side rims, or wall-mounted with concealed pipes. Some baths are supplied with tap holes, so make sure they are in the right position and of the type to suit your chosen taps.

Basins for general family washing should be at least 550mm (and preferably 600mm) wide by about 450mm deep. For adults the rim of the basin should be about 800mm off the floor. Materials which are used include acrylic, vitreous china or vitreous-enamelled steel.

There is a wide variety of shapes and styles – round, oval, geometric, shell shapes and so on. If space is limited, you can find wall-hung basins as little as 450mm wide by 230mm deep. There are basically three types of basin – pedestal, wall-hung and vanitory. Pedestal basins are in two parts, the basin itself being fixed to the wall, with the separate pedestal taking some of the weight and hiding unsightly supply and waste pipes.

Wall-hung basins are less expensive, take up less room and are easier to

Opposite The trend is towards larger fittings with well-defined, almost geometric profiles. *Below* Patterned fittings are back in fashion.

the rim of the bowl. Height to the top of the bowl is usually around 400mm. If space is at a premium, choose a slimline model measuring about 350mm in width. A close-coupled W.C., with bowl and cistern part of the same unit, is the neatest type.

There are two basic W.C. actions – wash-down and syphonic. The former has water flushing out from the rim, while the syphonic system sucks the water away, is more efficient and quieter, but also more expensive. The bowl can be either pedestal-style or wall-mounted.

Bidets can also be pedestal or wall-mounted. Allow 400mm for width and 600mm for projection from the wall to the rim of the bowl.

The simplest type of bidet is like a wash basin with water supply from taps. The type in which water pours from under the rim all around the bowl is more costly.

There are special taps for bidets, some including a pop-up waste instead of a plug and chain. Some bidet taps have a spray nozzle attached to make washing easier, but please be sure to check with your local Water Authority before you buy one in order to be absolutely certain that it doesn't contravene any of their bylaws.

install. They are fixed to the wall with strong brackets. The main drawback is that waste and supply pipes are left exposed.

Vanitory units can be pricey, but they hide all the plumbing, and provide storage space as well as useful surfaces around the basin. They are usually about 450mm to 575mm deep; widths vary from 600mm to about 1500mm for two-basin types.

W.C. sizes vary according to design but, generally, you should allow about 500mm for width, 800mm for height to the top of a low-level cistern and 700mm to 800mm for projection from the wall to

Right Pedestal basin: the pedestal hides the pipes as well as giving partial support to the basin.

Plumbing points

Any plans you make for your bathroom are limited by the degree to which you can adapt the plumbing facilities. The most crucial factor is the disposal of waste which, for obvious reasons of hygiene, is strictly covered by various inviolable regulations.

Waste from all the bathroom fittings is discharged via one or two soil pipes located on an external wall or internally in ducts. The soil pipes must be ventilated by a stack, a length of pipe running from the downpipe to a specified height above the roof eaves.

Soil pipes and stacks are very expensive to move, because they are connected directly into the drainage system and any alteration to this may well require considerable excavation as well as plumbing work. When planning bathroom improvements on a budget it is wise to assume that you're going to have to leave the existing soil pipe where it is, site the W.C. as close as possible to it, and lay out the rest of the new bathroom layout accordingly.

To avoid blockages, waste must flow under gravity into the downpipe. So, if fittings are situated some way from the discharge point, the pipe run will have to be angled to provide an adequate 'pull' to avoid blockages. Fittings should be no further than two metres (6ft 6in) from the soil pipe. In addition, fittings must have traps at about 10cm (4in) under the waste outlet to provide an initial drop into the waste pipe. These traps are water-sealed to prevent smells from escaping back into the room.

Basins and most W.C.s and bidets are usually high enough off floor level to allow a sufficient drop, but baths and showers can present problems. Many houses can accommodate bath and shower traps underneath the bathroom floor, but if this is impossible you will probably have to raise the floor area on which these fittings are situated.

The nearer the various waste outlets are to the external wall on which the soil pipes are situated, the less likelihood there is of blockages.

Ducted plumbing

In a well-planned bathroom *all* plumbing should be concealed. Pipes can be chased into the plaster or run behind plasterboard walls.

If these options present problems – because there is insufficient depth of plaster or a solid concrete floor, for example – you can use ducting. This is usually constructed from chipboard or plastic-faced plywood fixed on to a timber frame to leave a gap of 10cm (4in) between the real wall and the false one. Access must be provided to get to the pipes for repair work.

Expert advice

Finding a dependable plumber can be a problem. For any major job you should get two or three estimates from different firms, all of whom should belong to a recognized trade association such as the National Association of Plumbing, Heating and Mechanical Services Contractors. (Send a stamped, self-addressed envelope to the Association at 6 Gate Street, London WC2A 3HX, for a list of members in your area.)

Below How the plumbing works. Pipework for the water supply is concealed under floorboards, behind bath panels and inside a vanitory unit. The bath waste pipe, which must slope downwards, runs under floorboards and through the wall to the downpipes. The basin waste exits through the wall from inside the vanitory unit. The W.C.'s large-bore discharge pipe has only a short run, and then passes through the wall to the waste pipe.

Safety in the bathroom

Water and electricity are a potentially lethal combination, so great care must be taken in following the strict regulations which govern the use of electricity in the bathroom.

Electrical appliances, such as washing machines, tumble dryers and immersion heaters, can be installed in the bathroom but they must be wired into fused connection points, not plugged into 13-amp sockets. Switches must be out of reach of anyone using the bathroom fittings. Building these appliances into cupboards is safer and neater, but not essential, provided that all the regulations are followed. Electric heaters, such as oil-filled radiators are required, to be wired into fused connection units too.

The only portable electric appliance permitted in the bathroom is an electric shaver, which plugs into a special low-powered socket. No other socket outlets are allowed and extension leads must never be used to bring in any appliance.

Lights and infra-red heaters must have cord switches if the switch is positioned inside the bathroom. Heaters must be out of reach of anyone who is using the bath. Light bulbs must be fixed into enclosed bayonet fittings.

Room for a shower?

1 Cabinet in bronze-effect aluminium and smoked panels for a large, luxurious bathroom.
2 Elegantly finished shower at the end of a run of fitted wardrobes has its base laid below floor level.

3 There is often room in a bedroom corner for a shower cabinet.
4 A shower and basin in a teenager's room can do much towards shortening family queues for the bathroom!
5 Shower with a folding door is particularly economical for space.

6 The luxury of a dressing room is furthered by the addition of a shower.
7 An *en suite* shower room makes a practical alternative to a second bathroom.
8 Space-saving corner shower for a smaller bedroom.

9 Some showers are designed to blend in with period-style bedroom furniture.
10 Even a corner on a landing or above the stairs can provide usable space for a shower.
11 A small bedroom becomes pleasingly self-contained with a shower and vanitory unit.

Tiling a shower cubicle

The surface to be tiled should be reasonably flat, firm and free from dirt. First establish a level base (walls are rarely straight and cannot be used as a guide). Find the lowest point of the shower cubicle and make a mark one tile height above it. Draw a line passing through this point round the base of the cubicle, using a spirit level. To provide a base for the first row of tiles, fix wooden battens along the wall with the top edge touching the line (**1**). Check constantly with the spirit level.

Starting from the middle of the line, measure the number of tiles required at each side, marking the battens and allowing for the spacer lugs. Mark the position of the end tile (**2**) and fix a batten vertically at this point, using a plumb line and spirit level for accuracy. The first tile will be placed here (**3**).

Apply waterproof adhesive with a combed trowel about one square metre at a time (**4**). Begin with the bottom row of tiles and work upwards from the left-hand corner, pressing each tile firmly into place. Try to avoid sliding the tiles about.

Check levels constantly to prevent creeping. Pieces of thick card can be used to make minor adjustments in joints (**5**). Leave the battens until tiling is completed; then remove them and tile the spaces.

Ceramic tiles have a hard, glazed surface and a brittle backing. When cutting, keep the tile face upwards (**6**), score along the line to be cut and place a match underneath along the line. Press the edges of the tile down and it should snap cleanly. To fit irregular shapes, score as above and nip the surplus tile away with tile nippers (**7**). The cut edge should be smoothed with sandpaper.

Tiling around fixtures necessitates fiding a level base as before. Tiling proceeds upwards from the nearest full tile from the fixture, supported by a horizontal batten, with part-tiles fitted in later.

No sooner than 12 hours after fixing the tiles, mix waterproof grout, following the instructions given. Rub the grout well into the joints with a sponge to ensure complete penetration and then wipe off the excess with the sponge (**8**). Draw a thin, flat piece of wood, rounded at one end (such as an ice-lolly stick) along each joint. Finally, polish the surface with a dry cloth. You should allow the grouting to dry for 14 days before using the shower.

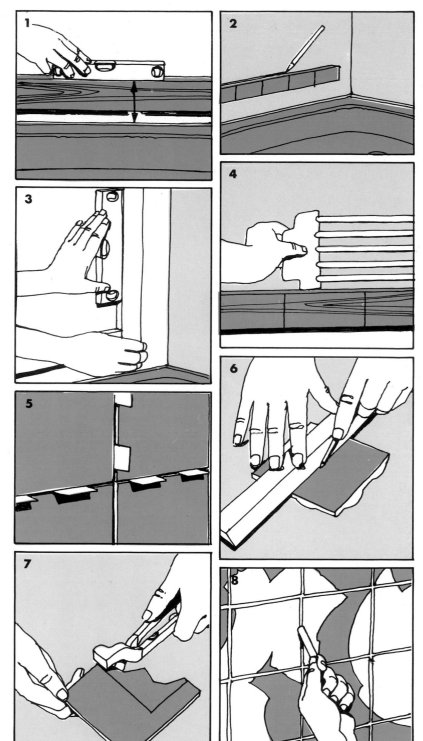

8.
THE BEDROOMS

The bedroom is just the place to let your personal taste in decor run riot – but it is a room, too, that benefits greatly from careful planning. Adequate storage space, for example, is vital if you wish to keep the room reasonably orderly. Furnishing, lighting and heating also need the same amount of attention as they get elsewhere in the house.

In most homes, the 'master' bedroom is easy to pick out – it's the biggest one. But is biggest necessarily best? Remember that a large room costs more to heat, and represents an awful lot of unused living area in the daytime.

If you are planning to move house, consider whether your new bedrooms might be more practically employed. Children, for example, would probably put a larger bedroom to much better use than you would; it would give them somewhere of their own to play during the day – which in itself could prove a real boon to you.

Whichever room you do choose as your own, it must at least be big enough to accommodate plenty of storage space, an easy chair and perhaps also a linen chest at the foot of the bed. Together with the usual essentials of dressing table, bedside tables and the bed itself, that is.

It is sometimes possible, particularly in houses with more bedrooms than are likely to be needed, to create that rare luxury, the bedroom suite. You might be able to achieve this by knocking through a dividing wall between a main bedroom and, say, a boxroom or a very small adjacent bedroom. The new room may be awkwardly shaped but, with a little ingenuity, this can be successfully utilized. The additional space could be an en suite bathroom or dressing room, or as in the drawing below, be used for the bed – leaving the rest of the room relatively uncluttered and therefore free for any purpose you choose.

While the bedroom with bathroom en suite is an ideal many of us yearn for, it is an expensive project and perhaps beyond the average budget. But you can go some of the way towards making the one bathroom more your own by fitting washbasins into the other bedrooms in

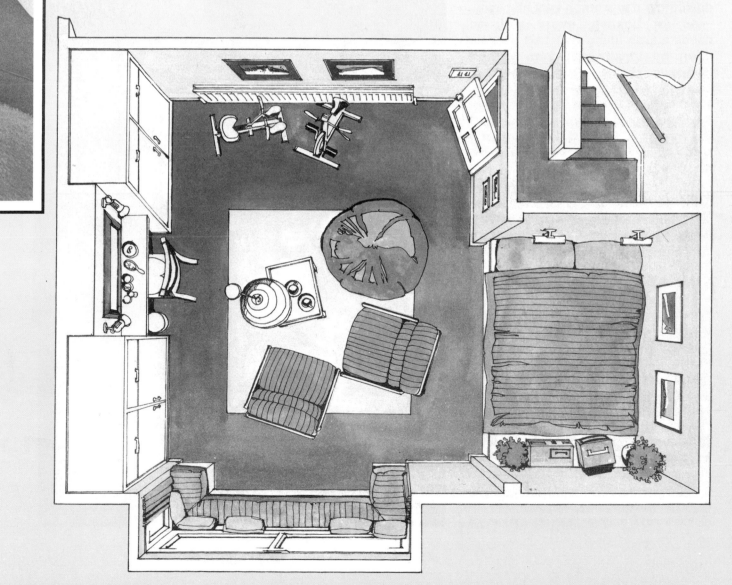

10.
DOWN TO BASICS:
CEILINGS

Renewing, repairing or even simply redecorating a ceiling can seem a daunting task. But in many homes – particularly older ones – ceilings in poor condition are a common let-down to the overall decorative appearance. Fortunately, working on ceilings is not as difficult a task as it might first appear.

Types of ceiling

Ceiling as architecture: a beautiful timber ceiling that plays rather more than the customary background role of ceilings in most of today's homes.

Lath and plaster ceilings, found only in older houses, consist of narrow timber strips nailed across the underside of the floor joists. Plaster is then applied to these laths and forced through the narrow gaps between them so that it squeezes out on the other side, forming a 'key' for the layer of plaster beneath. Finishing coats are then applied to this base layer.

These ceilings may sag over the years because laths come loose or the plaster key breaks up. Laths can be screwed back into place with galvanized (non-rusting) screws. If the laths are damaged and the key has gone, the laths can be cut back to the nearest joists and the gap filled with plasterboard nailed to the joists. This repair then needs a finishing coat of plaster to match it into the ceiling.

Applying a finishing skim of plaster over a wide area of ceiling is a skilled task. You should call in a professional to do any major job.

Plasterboard ceilings are universal in today's new homes. They simply comprise gypsum board nailed to the joists and finished with a coat of board-finish plaster. (A skilled craftsman, working with the right materials, doesn't even need the finish coat to produce a perfect surface.) Any sag in a plasterboard ceiling probably means the nails have loosened.

To find out whether your ceilings are the lath or the plasterboard type, climb into the loft and look between the floor joists. Plasterboard appears as a plain, flat surface, while a lath ceiling looks like lots of slats with blobs of plaster protruding between them. If loft access is a problem, lift a floorboard on the first floor and you'll be able to make the same inspection.

Suspended ceilings are simply false ceilings attached to the joists above and usually supported by perimeter battens attached to the walls. A suspended ceiling may serve to hide an old ceiling that cannot be repaired, or to 'lower' the ceiling to improve the look of an ill-proportioned room. Or it may act as translucent screen through which light from above can be dispersed evenly— and without shadow on to the room (usually a kitchen, bathroom or workroom).

There are a number of other types of ceilings, such as concrete and timber, but they are rarely found as standard features in modern houses. For repairs to such ceilings you would be well advised to seek professional help.

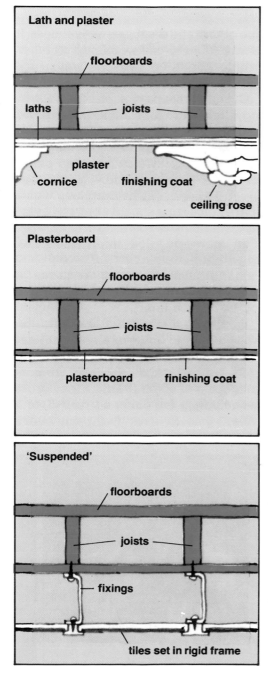

12.
DOWN TO BASICS: DECORATING GUIDE

With today's easy-to-use decorating materials and equipment, you need only modest skills to create a really first-class effect. Armed, too, with some very basic knowledge of interior design – plus the courage of your own convictions – you should be able to make some truly dramatic improvements to your rooms.

Colour is probably the most important factor to consider when home decorating. Not only can it alter the mood and feel of a room, making it appear warm or fresh, homely or elegant, but it also affects the feeling of dimension, even of size. And colour can change – or reflect – the moods and personalities of the people using the rooms: an important factor in choosing decorative schemes for rooms with differing purposes.

What *is* colour? Basically, it is light. The light we receive from the sun is white, made up of a spectrum of wavelengths of invisible colour, from infra-red to ultra-violet. If this light is passed through a prism, it is broken up and six colours from the light spectrum can be seen with the naked eye – red, orange, yellow, green, blue and violet. A rainbow is an example of this process; the sun's rays are reflected by falling raindrops, each one acting as a prism, which break up the light into the colours of the spectrum.

But the range of colours available is far greater than these six. In fact, the number of colours in the spectrum has been calculated at around ten million.

So it's hardly surprising that choosing colours for your home can be a little bewildering. It is helpful, therefore, if you understand colour and its effects – starting with the six main colours of the spectrum, which include red, yellow and blue, the primary colours from which all others derive.

Red Fiery, dramatic, eye-catching and exciting, red is associated with warmth and liveliness. It can be welcoming and cosy, but at the same time its psychological and physical effects quicken the pulse and prompt the release of adrenalin into the bloodstream, so it is also a stimulant. Red objects seem nearer than they actually are and we react much more quickly to red than to any other colour.

Orange is very much an earthy colour. Through all its hues from pale apricot to deep, burnt orange, it represents nature: golden autumn leaves, warm sunsets and fresh fruit. It gives a feeling of solidity, warmth, serenity and reassurance. Orange can be cheerful and stimulating like red, but also tends to be tiring and slightly irritating in large, concentrated quantities.

Minuet 2

Kingcup 182*

Coronet 97*

Vermont 371

Right The toning colours of yellow and green make an eye-catching scheme that all fits naturally together.

Hornpipe 169*

Nantucket 233†

-he 111

Ballerina 31†

Rosebud 294†

Kou

Cleopatra 85

9*

Yokohama 398†

Sodapop 322*

Limehouse 188*

-bird 170*

Halcyon 16

Bengal 34*

Lomond 192*

Lucerne 196

Flame 137*

Pimento 268

iance 278†

Sugarcane 3

Pansy 253

Teazle 346†

Aconite 3†

Archduk

ou 15*

Peony 263*

ade 309†

Caledonia 55

inette 16

Be sure to follow the manufacturers' instructions – and notes on the safety of some cement-based products – very closely.

Grout Use waterproof grout wherever necessary, as ordinary grout has little resistance to dirt and moisture. Grout is available either as a white, cement-based powder for mixing with water, or ready-mixed. It can be coloured with powder colorants or liquid tints normally sold for paint.

Preparing New plaster needs six months to dry out before you can tile it. Old plaster should be clean, sound and free of damp (fill cracks and holes with cellulose filler and smooth). Apply a coat of stabilizing primer to very porous plaster.

All old wall coverings must be stripped away to reveal the plaster. Old paint should be sanded to give adhesive a good grip; any flaking paint must be scraped away.

Poor or exceptionally uneven walls are best covered before tiling, and dry lining is the best method – with the added merits of reducing condensation and perhaps concealing exposed pipework.

One useful technique is to fix 50-mm (2-in) square battens vertically to the wall at 400-mm (16-in) intervals, employing screws and wallplugs. Cover with plasterboard, fixing additional horizontal battens as and when required in order to support the joins between the plasterboard sheets (see drawing at top, right).

Where there are existing tiles, you may find that you are able to tile over them, but where the grouting between the old and the new tiles does not coincide, you will probably get some unevenness. It is generally better, therefore, to remove the old tiles using a club hammer and cold chisel (second illustration from the top). Unfortunately, plaster may tend to chip off the wall together with the old adhesive.

Setting out To find the starting place you will need a gauge rod. To make one, lay out a row of tiles on the floor, set 3mm ($\frac{1}{8}$in) apart if they don't have spacer lugs or bevels, and mark the position of the joins on a straight timber batten 1.22m (4ft) long (as shown below). Continue each marking right round the batten with the aid of a try square.

Finding the horizontal Hold the gauge rod vertically against the wall. Then work out the positions of the horizontal rows by transferring lightly in pencil the join marks from the gauge rod to the wall. It's unlikely that an exact number of tiles will fit. A gap less than 6mm ($\frac{1}{4}$in) can be filled with grout, preferably at the top of the wall.

If the gap is larger, centre the rows of whole tiles to give equal rows top and bottom; cut tiles should be at least 25mm (1in), as less is difficult to cut.

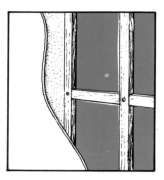

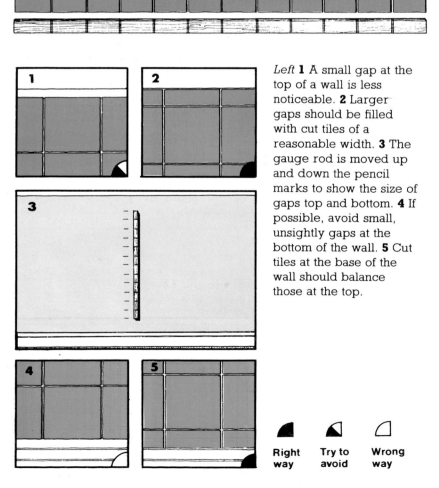

Left **1** A small gap at the top of a wall is less noticeable. **2** Larger gaps should be filled with cut tiles of a reasonable width. **3** The gauge rod is moved up and down the pencil marks to show the size of gaps top and bottom. **4** If possible, avoid small, unsightly gaps at the bottom of the wall. **5** Cut tiles at the base of the wall should balance those at the top.

Right way   **Try to avoid**   **Wrong way**

As for the rest, the most popular is stone. It might be carved for monumental effect, left rough for rustic charm or laid randomly to create the sort of fireplace you might expect in a Wild West log cabin. Different structures may be modestly modern or huge, like continental chimney breasts.

Various stones are used, each of which will give the design its own particular character. Marble and slate are the most expensive. Attractive alternatives are York (a grey/brown sandstone), Cotswold (a creamy yellow limestone), Purbeck (a marble lookalike) and Derby (a brown, flinty millstone grit). Granite is also popular.

Brick, either genuine or in the form of thin, tile-like briquettes, is widely used, too, particularly in rustic fireplaces and in the less flamboyant modern styles.

Finally, don't forget the unashamedly modern fireplaces. You'll find delightfully simple 'hole in the wall' designs, stylish, space-age freestanding models in metal and any number of types built more or less conventionally but tailored to suit the user's particular needs.

Expert advice To be sure you buy from a reputable dealer and use a qualified expert for installation, you should deal with a member of the National Fireplace Council. To obtain your nearest members' names and addresses, contact the Council at PO Box 35, Stoke on Trent, Staffs ST4 7NU. Their members ensure that the work conforms to current safety regulations and the building regulations.

If you are making alterations to any fireplace, you will probably need Building Regulations Approval, so check with your local council's Building Control Officer.

Make sure you have the information you need when shopping around for a fireplace. It is best to draw up a plan of the room, with dimensions, including ceiling height. Note the position of the chimney breast with its dimensions both inside and outside the house. Also note the depth, width and height of the existing fireplace opening. You should, in addition, mark the positions of doors, windows, radiators, gas points, power sockets and fixtures.

Choosing the style A great many fireplaces available today are reproductions of period pieces, generally comprising carved wooden mantelpieces with a marble, stone, brick or tile infill. There are also a few cast-iron models to choose from.

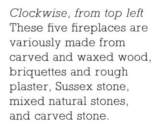

Clockwise, from top left
These five fireplaces are variously made from carved and waxed wood, briquettes and rough plaster, Sussex stone, mixed natural stones, and carved stone.

A style to fit

If you are restoring a period room to its former glory, it's vital to choose a fireplace that fits in. Does the fireplace have such a strong character that it will look wrong if you alter the way the room is decorated or furnished? Is it too small to fulfil its role as a focal point? Or worse: is it so large that everything else is dwarfed beside it?

Make sure you know the answers to all these questions before you reach a final decision on which type of new fireplace to install, or on how to redecorate a room around an existing one.

From Adam-style (top right) to a gleaming new stove set in a modern tiled fireplace (right) and Victorian reproduction (left) every style has its own attractions.

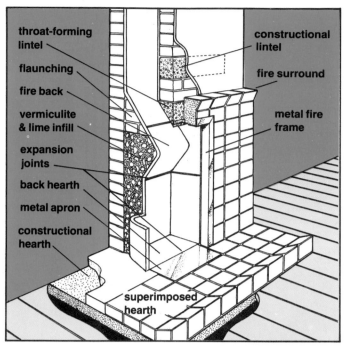

throat-forming lintel
flaunching
fire back
vermiculite & lime infill
expansion joints
back hearth
metal apron
constructional hearth
constructional lintel
fire surround
metal fire frame
superimposed hearth

Left A section of a typical fireplace showing the various features. But remember that individual fireplaces do differ in construction.

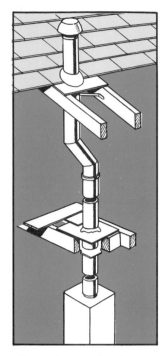

Above A new flue is easily installed using a prefabricated chimney system. The diagram shows the floor and roof levels and the interlocking parts of this pipe system. These slot together in much the same way as modern guttering systems.

Left The builder's opening. This is what you should be left with when you strip an old fireplace in preparation for a fresh start.

Fitting a new fireplace

Replacing an existing fireplace should be a fairly simple, if laborious task. The diagram above shows a typical construction.

First job is to remove the surround and hearth (see opposite), and in many cases this will be all the preparation that's required. A new heating appliance will often slot into the existing fireback, which can then be finished off by adding the new surround. The manufacturer often gives instructions for you to do this yourself.

There are situations in which you will need to remove the old fireback as well and build up the new fireplace from what's called the builder's opening (see diagram above). This will be necessary if the new appliance won't fit, but it should also be done if the existing fireback is damaged or if there is a back boiler. This, too, will probably need replacing or at least repositioning to suit the new fire.

Unless a back boiler is involved, you should be able to remove the fireback yourself. Chisel away the flaunching at the top of the back, lever out the fireclay and remove all the infill. Rebuilding the back is a more skilled task, however, since this will have a marked effect on the general efficiency of the new fire. It is therefore worthwhile having this done professionally.

Unblocking a bricked-in fireplace can be done with a club hammer and cold chisel, but be sure there is a fireplace behind it. In an upstairs room, a chimney breast may be the continuation of the flue from a downstairs fire.

The depth of the chimney breast is a good guide. If it is deeper than about 350mm (14in) it may well contain a fireplace. You can also count the number of chimney pots, as there should be one per fireplace.

Starting from scratch If your home has neither existing fireplaces nor flues, don't despair. Thanks to modern pre-fabricated chimney systems, this isn't as vast an undertaking as you might think. There are, basically, two systems to choose from. In the first, precast blocks can be built up either outside or inside the house to form a chimney. The second comprises metal pipes which are assembled rather like the components used in modern guttering. A precast block chimney can be decorated like any other masonry.

Removing an old fireplace and surround

1 The fire surround will usually be fitted to the wall by screws and fixing lugs buried beneath the plaster.

2 After having removed the surround, lever up the decorative, superimposed hearth using a spade and timber wedges.

3 To remove the fireback, first chop out the flaunching that forms the slope which goes up into the flue.

4 The old broken fireback, together with any loose infill found behind it, can now be removed with a shovel.

Opening up a disused chimney

1 Many were blocked with plywood or hardboard tacked on to a wood frame. The skirting board must be removed, too.

2 Bricks or concrete blocks, plastered over, must be removed with a club hammer and cold chisel.

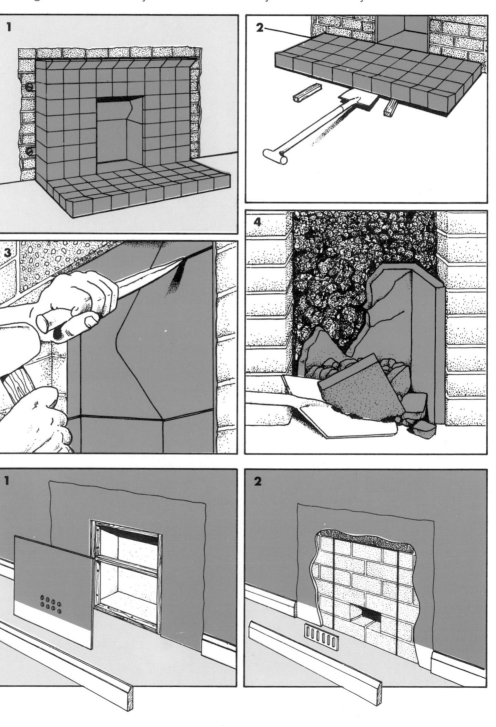

14.
DOWN TO BASICS: INSULATION

Without adequate insulation, no home is either comfortable or economic to live in. Heating costs being as high as they are, and winter temperatures being as low, good insulation is a sound investment which in many cases will pay for itself in saved fuel charges within a year of installation. Among all home improvements, insulation is therefore one of the most vital – and one of the few that pays for itself.

If last year your heating bills were high, it might not only have been the dismal weather that was responsible. Taking a typical prewar house as an example, without insulation it might have cost around £250 for gas central heating. With full insulation, that bill could have been cut by about £100. If the house has heating based on other, more expensive fuels, the saving would have been proportionately greater.

Your insulation strategy Full insulation is in itself costly so, although you should bear it in mind as your ultimate goal, you may do better in the short term to arrive at a more modest insulation policy that is effective without being financially out of reach.

According to the Department of Energy, the heat loss from a typical semi-detached home divides up as follows: 25% through the roof; 35% through the walls; 10% through windows; 15% through doors and 15% through the floors. In each area, there is much you can do to reduce this heat loss. (Note, however, that these figures are for a semi-detached house. In other kinds of houses the proportions may well be different.)

Before going ahead with a particular form of insulation, weigh the cost against the likely benefits to ensure that you get the best possible value for money – in other words, a good return on your investment.

Pitched roofs As the roof is responsible for about a quarter of the average home's heat loss, it should come high on your list of priorities, particularly when you consider that insulating it need be neither expensive nor difficult. As long as you can get into the loft, and provided you do not intend using it for anything more than occasional storage, there is no need to touch the roof itself.

There are several materials you can use, but the most common of these is glass fibre blanket. This comes in rolls about 5m (16ft) long and 400mm (15in) wide and is laid between the joists. You should allow a minimum thickness of 100mm (4in).

Another material is loose-fill insulant that you pour between the joists and level off to the required depth. Vermiculite, a granular mineral-based product, is the most widely available but polystyrene beads or loose mineral fibre can also be used. All are very effective in situations where you cannot fit glass fibre blanket between the joists, and they also offer a convenient method of topping up existing insulation.

Some loose-fill materials, however, tend to be less effective than glass fibre blanket, so a thicker layer is needed to give comparable results: 150mm (6in) of Vermiculite is equivalent to 100mm (4in) of glass fibre, which usually means covering the joists. Also, loose fills are lightweight – polystyrene particularly – and may get blown into drifts if the loft is very draughty, leaving costly gaps in the insulation.

You can get someone in to do the job for you. Many small local builders will tackle this sort of work at a reasonable price, using more or less the same methods and materials as you would if you were doing the job yourself. If you call in a firm that specializes in insulation, you can expect to obtain a worthwhile guarantee against any future problems.

Some specialist firms may suggest pumping loose fibre into the loft using a special machine. This form of insulation is especially useful if the design of your loft makes conventional insulation difficult; it should also work out cheaper. However, you should watch out for firms offering to insulate your loft with the same sort of foam which is used in cavity wall filling. It is unsuitable.

If your storage requirements make it impractical to insulate the loft floor, you should look at ways to insulate the roof itself. The simplest option is to put glass fibre blanket between the rafters, where it may hold itself in place. If it does not, either devise some method of fixing it – a few carefully placed battens nailed to the rafter will do – or use a glass fibre blanket designed for the purpose. Generally this will be sandwiched between sheets of heavy building paper which can be nailed or stapled to the rafters. Alternatively, you can insulate with blocks of polystyrene cut to fit tightly between the rafters. But this can be expensive.

If you cannot get adequate access to the space between rafters, you could simply try glass fibre blanket stapled in place, if looks are unimportant. Or, where you are dealing with a habitable attic room, you could choose one of the various systems used to insulate solid walls.

Occasionally it is possible to pour a loose-fill insulant into the space between covered-over rafters, and this should prove far cheaper. However, you must make sure that the material does not just pour out of the bottom, especially if there is a risk of it blocking up the eaves. Glass fibre can irritate the skin, so wear a mask and gloves if you use it.

Flat roofs usually waste even more heat than pitched ones. They are trickier to insulate and it is extremely doubtful whether the resulting saving would justify the cost.

This is certainly true of existing flat roofs. You must either virtually rebuild them to put in the necessary 100mm (4in) of glass fibre blanket – or its equivalent – or you must add some sort of false ceiling and insulate above it. You would probably do better to confine yourself merely to curing the condensation problems for which flat roofs are notorious, possibly by putting up a warm decorative ceiling treatment such as polystyrene tiles. Technically, this is a form of insulation, but don't expect to see any significant reduction in your fuel bills.

If you have a flat roof that is due for extensive repairs, check with your roofing contractor to find out if it can be insulated at the same time. This would be about the only economic method of doing the job.

Walls are responsible for as much as one-third of heat loss, but whether or not they are worth insulating depends on how they are built.

Right Step-by-step in the loft. **1** Cover loft floor with polythene sheeting to prevent condensation in insulation. **2** Roll out glass fibre blanket, trimming it to fit snugly. **3** Carry insulation to the eaves but don't block them. **4** Don't forget the trap door. **5** and **6** Lag all exposed pipes. **7** and **8** Use either polystyrene sheets or a casing filled with insulant to protect tank, but don't insulate under it.

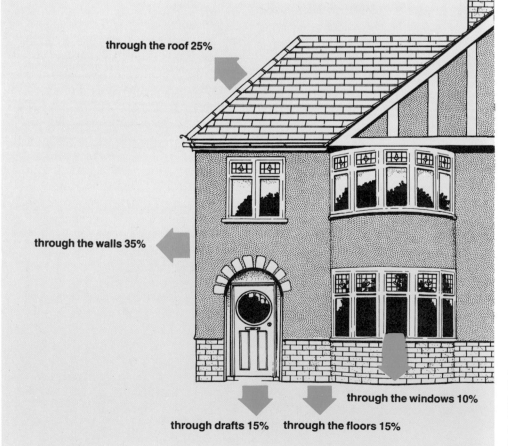

through the roof 25%

through the walls 35%

through the windows 10%

through drafts 15%   through the floors 15%

Left The kinds of heat loss typical from various parts of a semi-detached house – giving some idea of the priorities and options you have in terms of insulation.

Cavity walls should be insulated by a specialist contractor, who can guarantee the job for at least 25 years. Use a company that is a member of the National Cavity Insulation Association or at least check that the system they use has an Agrément Certificate. As additional insurance against problems, make certain that the installer has got permission from the local authority before starting work.

Materials used include UFoam (the cheapest), mineral fibre, plastic beads and polyurethane foam (the most expensive). You should discuss with the contractor the different merits of these materials in relation to your own particular needs.

Bearing in mind the ultimate savings on your heating bills if you can afford cavity wall insulation (at around £600 for an average semi), it is well worth having. It should pay for itself within three to four years.

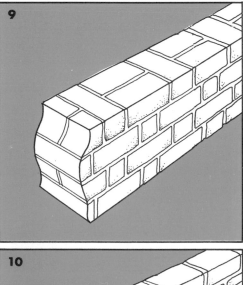

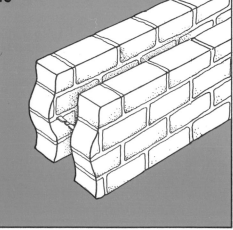

Far right Solid walls (**9**) can be easily identified by the half bricks visible on the wall's face. Cavity walls (**10**) have two leaves with an air gap between. They are usually laid in a pattern called stretcher bond.

If the brickwork is visible, look at how the bricks are arranged or 'bonded'. Cavity walls are almost invariably in stretcher bond and solid walls are not. If the brickwork is concealed, get into the loft and examine the tops of the walls. If there is a cavity, you should be able to see it from above.

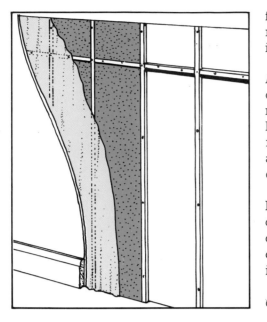

Solid walls lose more heat than cavity walls, but insulating them is difficult. Insulating the outside is a professional job involving covering the wall with blocks of material and protecting it with rendering or cladding – at a cost of perhaps £3000 for a semi.

Inside, insulation is a little easier. The simplest method is to line the walls with insulated plasterboard, sticking it in place with a special adhesive. Alternatively, you can cover the walls with a series of battens, lay insulation between them, then cover with polythene sheeting and finally with plasterboard, chipboard or timber cladding. The cost is around £500 for a semi if you do it yourself, perhaps £800 if you employ a professional – plus, of course, the cost of redecorating the whole house afterwards!

Floors New solid floors should be made with insulation incorporated in the form of a dense polystyrene foam layer between the base floor and the screed or chipboard surface. But this is scarcely worth doing to an existing floor. You would be better advised to pay a little extra for a good thick carpet and underlay.

Much the same applies to suspended floors, except that you can lift the floorboards and insulate with glass fibre blanket draped over the joists, avoiding the necessity of raising the

floor level. Again, for the effort and results, a good carpet is a better investment.

Draught-proofing is undoubtedly one of the best possible insulation investments. You can draught-proof your own home probably for less than £40 and recover the whole cost within 12 months as well as gaining immeasurably in comfort.

Remember, though, that some ventilation is vital – so don't try to eliminate draughts completely. Limit your draught-proofing measures to external doors, windows and the trap door leading into the loft.

And take care when choosing products. Foam draught-strips are cheap

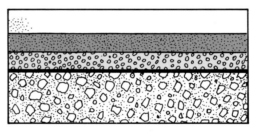

and suitable for rarely used windows and doors. In most other places, however, they wear out very quickly. Instead, you need a rigid plastic or metal weather-strip or a draught-strip with a rubber gap filler and a rigid body. Brush draught-strips and draught-proofing constructed with silicon mastics are also long-lasting and effective products.

There are some areas where even these items will be ineffective – such as at sash windows, gaps beneath doors and letter-box flaps, for example. You will find a variety of draught-excluders which are specifically intended for these places and, at the front door especially, it is well worth paying out for a product that will last.

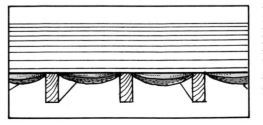

Far left Insulating an inside wall: you will need a frame of timber battens, insulating material, polythene sheeting and plasterboard to cover.

Left Cross-section of an insulated solid floor. From top: concrete screed or chipboard, insulation, damp-proof membrane and existing base floor.

Left Suspended timber floors can be insulated by laying glass fibre blanket over the joists, with polythene sheeting above, then replacing the floorboards.

Damp and condensation

Even if you ignore the health risks associated with damp, you cannot escape its destructive powers. A mild attack is sufficient to ruin decor, while a more serious outbreak can encourage wet or dry rot as well as the attentions of wood-devouring insects. Ultimately, your home's structural timberwork is at risk – with potentially disastrous results.

Essentially, there are five causes of damp outbreaks: namely, rising damp,

Right Most damp is due to physical defects in your home. Illustrated are some of the most common.

Loose or damaged roofing
Blocked, leaking or ill-fitted gutters
Cracked or blistered rendering
Damaged brick and pointing
Paving too close to dpc

penetrating damp, dampness which is due to faulty plumbing or guttering, 'new building' damp and damp caused by condensation.

Rising damp is the moisture absorbed by building materials from the ground. In newer homes a damp-proof course (dpc) of bricks or a layer of slate prevent this moisture rising to where it can do damage, but in older houses this may be absent. Walls lacking a dpc can usually be treated by making one or two courses waterproof, which involves saturating them with chemicals pumped in under pressure through holes drilled in the masonry. An alternative method is to cut a slot right round the house between two courses of brickwork and insert a barrier such as roofing felt, zinc or slate. This can prove expensive but is likely to be considerably more durable than a chemical dpc.

Whichever you choose, have it installed by a reputable contractor – the system should have an Agrément Certificate – and be sure you get a worthwhile guarantee. Take care never to 'bridge' a dpc with, say, a pile of sand placed against the house. The moisture will travel quickly into the upper part of the wall.

Damp-proofing an old solid floor means digging it up and rebuilding it. With less drastic remedies such as using bitumen emulsion or a waterproof flooring laid on waterproof adhesive, you risk encouraging rising damp in the walls. It may be best simply to choose a flooring which allows the damp to evaporate, such as quarry tiles.

Penetrating damp can occur when the air gap in a cavity wall is 'bridged' by mortar deposits on the ties linking the outer and inner walls. On the whole this affects mainly new buildings and can be spotted because the damp patches are often regularly spaced at the tie points.

But penetrating damp is commoner in solid walls, particularly those on exposed sites or facing prevailing winds. Pointing and rendering therefore need careful upkeep and damaged bricks

Left Widespread damp and mould in the loft are commonly due to condensation. Leaks tend to produce more localized damage.

Below The sooty deposit on this ceiling is a fungus caused by condensation. Note how it avoids the line of the warmer joists.

Far right Rising damp is the prime suspect for mould at ground floor level, though in hidden corners condensation may be to blame.

should be replaced. In order to achieve extra protection, you can waterproof the surface either with exterior paint or a clear silicon waterproofing compound.

In a basement or elsewhere without external-wall access the best solution is to line the walls with a bitumen-impregnated sheeting such as Newtonite and cover this with plasterboard.

Faulty plumbing and guttering may be responsible for damp patches, so check gutters for leaks by pouring water into them on a dry day. Leaks from pipes which are buried in walls may look like penetrating damp, but you will soon be able to spot the difference, because plumbing leaks don't stop when the sun shines.

If the pipes in your home are of the old lead type, they should all be replaced – before the inevitable day when leaks become general and do some real damage to your furnishings and decorations.

New building damp Concrete, plaster, mortar and so on have a high water content when mixed and, although most of these materials dry out quickly during hardening, the structure actually takes over six months to 'cure' properly. In the interim, new surfaces should not be decorated with impervious wall coverings (such as vinyl) but with cheap materials that will allow the structure to dry out.

Condensation is the damp that forms on cold surfaces in rooms where the air is warm and moist. In theory, to combat condensation you simply provide warm surfaces: everything from double-glazing to cork floors. In practice, to cure condensation you also have to stop the air reaching saturation point. So you either heat the air to increase its moisture-carrying potential or reduce the amount of moisture available to be carried by it.

The first option may sound expensive in fuel bills, but in fact the best policy is to provide low-level heating round the clock in order to prevent the house from ever becoming too cold, which might

save fuel anyway. As for reducing moisture, if you do have condensation troubles, you must take steps to improve ventilation. In a bathroom or laundry room this may mean fitting a powered extractor fan; in a kitchen a cooker hood may be needed. In other rooms it may be sufficient to open the windows regularly.

Condensation is probably the commonest of all causes of damp inside the home, so if you do discover patches, particularly on bathroom and kitchen walls, don't just assume it's penetrating damp. Remember that rising and penetrating damp are worse during or after rain, while condensation can strike at any time, most noticeably on cold or muggy days.

Finally . . . Once you have cured your damp problems, be sure to kill any mould that accompanied the dampness. Mildew and black sooty moulds can be dealt with by removing any wall covering, scrubbing the surface clean, then treating with a fungicide. Rotten timber is more serious and should be dealt with professionally.

Remember that dampness will not disappear overnight. A solid wall, for example, may take between six and nine months to dry out.

15.
DOWN TO BASICS:
WINDOWS

Good looking windows work wonders for the appearance of
your home from the outside, and they do a lot for your comfort
inside. If , on the other hand, your existing windows are
dilapidated you probably have trouble with draughts, worries
about security – and a very dreary-looking home. Window
improvements, therefore, are a real priority.

Because your windows need attention that doesn't mean they need replacing. New windows, especially double-glazed ones, can be expensive, so first decide whether some basic repairs are really all that's needed. Here are some of the commonest problems, and how to remedy them:

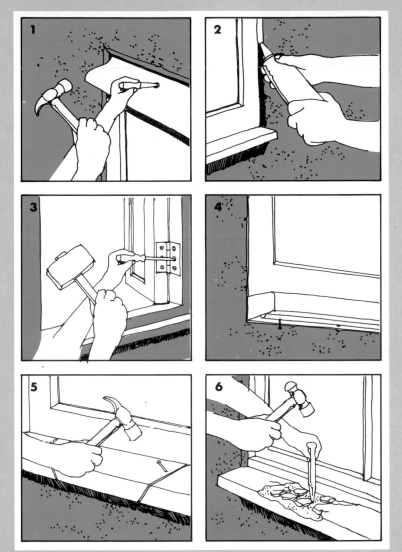

1 Rotten drip moulding. Prise off the old and replace with the same type (you may have to order it), fixing the new length with nails punched home and their heads covered with filler.

2 Gap between wall and frame should be filled with a mastic sealer, straight from the tube.

3 Loose hinges. If screws will not grip, take them out, push in small pieces of wood such as matchsticks and try again. Or use new screws $\frac{1}{4}$in or $\frac{1}{2}$in longer, and of the same diameter (usually no. 10).

A broken hinge must be replaced. If you have difficulty removing the old screws because their slots are clogged with paint, scrape off as much as possible, place the blade of a plastic-handled screwdriver in the slot and give the handle a sharp tap with a mallet. Don't be too heavy handed, though, lest you crack the glass. The screw should then turn. Repeat if necessary until it does.

4 Blocked drip channel. Scrape out paint and dirt to clear it. If there is no channel, you can make one by pinning a length of half-round moulding under the sill.

5 Rotting timber sill. Not an easy job: Remove rotted section by sawing then chopping with chisel and mallet. Cut a new timber to fit and wood-glue into place. Drive nails through the top and at an angle so that they go into the existing sill on each side.

6 Damaged concrete sill. Use a bolster and hammer to chip off loose top surface of sill to a depth of 40mm (1$\frac{1}{2}$in). Mix mortar of three to one sand and cement. Dampen the top of the sill and place a batten at the front to act as a frame. Trowel in the mortar, and smooth it level with the top of the batten. Smooth off the top with a float.

the right cord length for the outer sash measure the distance from the top of the sash to the bottom of the cord groove and mark it on the frame. Pull the cord so the weight is clear of the bottom of the compartment and cut the cord level with the mark (**7**). Tie a large knot in the end of the cord so the weight cannot pull it over the pulley. Do the same for an inner sash, except that the mark on the frame should be level with the bottom of the cord groove when the sash is closed. Pull the cord until the weight is just below the pulley, and cut level with the mark (**8**). Nail the cords in the grooves (**9**), leaving the top couple of inches free of nails.

Repairing a sash window A window that rattles or sticks may need adjustment to the beadings that form the channel in which it runs. To reduce or widen the channel for the inner sash, use an old chisel to prise out the staff (inner) beads (**1**) and refix them appropriately, using new pins. To alter the width of the channel for the outer sash, you must prise out and reposition the stop (outer) beads as well as the staffs (**2**). Damaged beads can be replaced, but take a sample to the timber merchant to be sure you buy the same profile. Fix with new pins (**3**).

If a cord needs renewing, the chances are the rest will soon need replacing, too, so consider fitting new cord all round if one has broken. Prise out the staff bead, swing the inner sash clear (**4**), take the nails out where they hold the cord in the side grooves and remove the sash from the opening. Prise out the parting bead and remove the outer sash similarly. Prise out the pocket, pull the weight out (**5**) and discard the cord tied to it. Clear debris from the compartment. Take a small weight tied to a length of string, the other end of which is tied to your new sash cord, and pass the weight over the pulley (**6**) into the compartment. Ease the cord into reach and tie it to the sash weight. To get

Reglazing a timber window Wearing gloves, score all round the broken pane with a glass cutter (**1**) then, with a hammer, gently tap out the panel (**2**), removing the glass carefully. Finally tap and lever out the pieces that remain at the edges. Use an old chisel to remove all the putty from the rebate (the angle of the frame in which the glass sits). Pull out the old glazing sprigs with pincers and dust out with a brush. Knead the putty until it is soft, then press it into the rebate all round (**3**). Place the new pane in position and gently press it into place. On the outside of the pane, tap in glazing sprigs, at least one every 300mm (12in). You can use the edge of a chisel for this (**4**) as a hammer in unpractised hands might break the glass. Place more putty on the outside of the pane and smooth it with a putty knife (**5**). Aim for a neat mitre at the corners (**6**). This is really the only difficult part of the whole operation, so take your time over it. The putty should come just below the level of the inside edge of the rebate so it cannot be seen from inside the house (**7**). Finally, run an old paint brush lightly over the putty, to seal it to the glass. When the putty has hardened in a week or so, paint it, taking the paint line about 3mm (⅛in) on to the glass level with the top of the rebate to form a watertight seal.

Metal-framed windows are dealt with in much the same way, but you need a special putty and you use clips (**8**) instead of glazing sprigs. Reglazing sliding metal windows, especially patio doors, is a job for a professional.

Buying glass Take great care to measure accurately. The glass should be 3mm (⅛in) less all round than the opening, and you should allow for the depth of the groove cut into the upper part of many frames. Be sure to tell the glass merchant for what purpose the new pane is intended: different thicknesses of glass are required for glazing different types and sizes of windows.

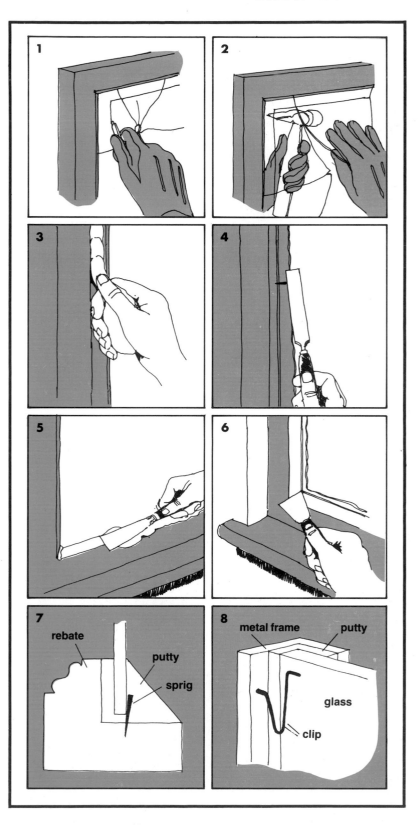

7 rebate — putty — sprig

8 metal frame — putty — glass — clip

Double glazing traps air between two sheets of glass, and this air is very effective in stopping heat and noise. How effective depends on how still the trapped air is and on whether or not it can escape from between the sheets of glass. This is the first aspect to consider when choosing double glazing. Basically, there are two options.

The most effective method is to have both panes mounted in a single, ordinary window frame – a system called sealed unit double glazing. This has two advantages: you can operate the window for ventilation as easily as if it were single-glazed and the air that is held between the panes is well and truly trapped.

The alternative is secondary glazing, which means that the extra pane of glass is mounted in a separate frame. To open a window you have, in effect, to open two. Coupled with the difficulty of getting a perfect seal between window frames and walls, this means that secondary glazing is likely to be much less effective than true double glazing.

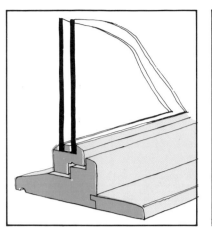 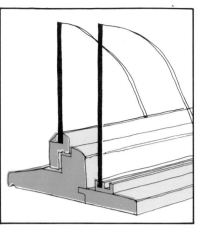

Is double glazing good value for money? As a form of insulation, double glazing will take a long time to pay for itself in terms of reduced fuel bills, but it will make a significant contribution to the comfort of your home by cutting draughts. And not just those that get through gaps: double glazing reduces the down draught of cold air caused by contact with cold windows because the inner pane is warmer than it would be with single glazing.

Above left Double glazing traps a layer of air between panes in a sealed unit.
Above right Existing windows can be supplemented by installing secondary glazing.

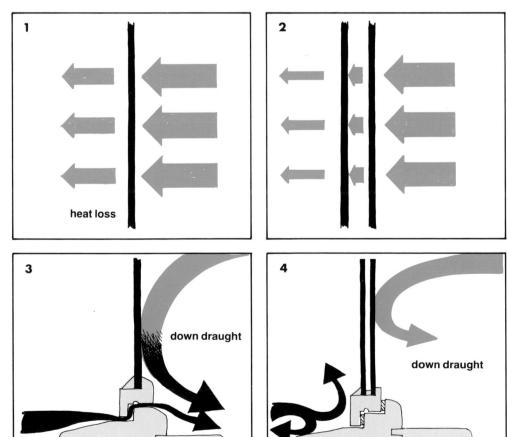

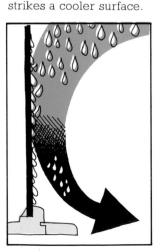

Left **1** A great deal of heat is lost through a single pane. **2** Double glazing reduces heat loss by as much as half. **3** Air creeps in through the frame to combine with the down draught. **4** Down draught is reduced by double glazing and draught-proofing.
Below Condensation occurs when warm air strikes a cooler surface.

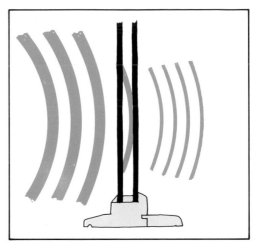

Right Sound waves penetrate single glazing quite easily.
Far right Double glazing cuts noise – and the wider the gap the more the noise is reduced.

If your existing windows are in need of replacement, then double glazing is well worth considering, because it is not necessarily that much more expensive than single-glazed replacement windows.

When choosing double glazing, note that the thickness of the layer of air trapped between the panes is important. Too small a gap between panes means there is not enough air to do the job. Too big a gap allows the trapped air to circulate, carrying heat from the inner to the outer pane. For maximum efficiency, a 19-mm gap is recommended. (This is not easy to achieve with secondary glazing.)

Double glazing tends to reduce the problem of condensation, because the inside pane remains comparatively warm. However, double glazing can *cause* condensation in the home by cutting off all draughts, so good ventilation is important. Secondary glazing can suffer condensation problems, too, because moisture-laden air tends to get into the gap, where it cools and condenses just as if the window had been double-glazed. You can buy special moisture-absorbing crystals to place between the panes in order to reduce this condensation. Any sealed double glazing unit that suffers this problem, incidentally, should be returned to the manufacturer.

If you intend installing double glazing to reduce noise rather than heat loss, a large air gap is needed: at least 100mm (4in) and ideally 200mm (8in). The only way you are likely to manage this is with secondary glazing in a deep window reveal, but it will be very effective indeed.

As well as having double glazing fitted by a manufacturer/installer, remember that you can do much of the work yourself and save money. Ask about DIY kits at your local builder's merchant or glazing specialist.

Far right If you're making your own double glazing and find that the rebate is fractionally too thin, simply fit one pane in front of the glazing bead. Cut a step in the bead for a firm fit.

Far right Typical construction of a sealed unit – either factory- or home-made.

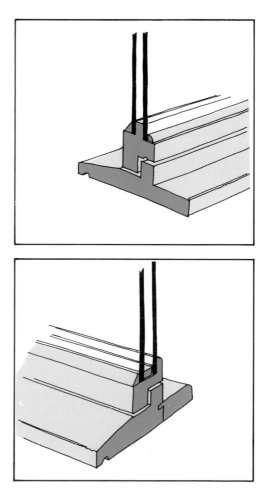

Replacement windows Since there is little point in paying for two window frames when one will do, double glazing for replacement windows means sealed units. What you need to consider, therefore, is the type of window frame.

The cheapest are in softwood, available in a variety of standard styles, from modern to the more traditional. Their main drawback is that they must be painted regularly to stand up to the weather. They will last from about 10 to 20 years.

In the long term, pricier hardwood windows are a better bet. They are normally varnished in order to highlight the wood's natural beauty and are better made than the average softwood window.

Next come steel windows, available in a limited range of modern styles or in those reminiscent of other periods. Regular painting is advisable if you want steel windows to last.

Aluminium windows are more popular. Most have a matt metallic anodized finish but colours are available. Period styles are made. Some have a mock leaded light effect – the 'lead' is in the air gap. Aluminium windows are fairly expensive, particularly if you opt for a brand that has efficient draught-proofing and some sort of insulation barrier in the frame itself.

Aluminium does not rot, but the windows are always installed with a timber sub-frame. Even a durable hardwood used for this purpose will have to be varnished every few years to keep it in good condition.

Finally, there are the newest type of replacement windows: uPVC or rigid plastic. These are very sophisticated, and not to be confused with simple plastic secondary panes. Rot-proof, colour-fast (they are normally white) and strong, they are easy to keep clean and, unlike aluminium, are fixed direct to the masonry; there is no sub-frame. As you might expect for such a product, uPVC windows are not cheap. They are about the same price as the more expensive aluminium types.

Patio doors Apart from windows, the other feature of the home that's worth double glazing is the patio door.

Hardwood, aluminium and plastic units for double glazing patio doors have similar pros and cons as for windows. Choose carefully from the security point of view, too, because some patio doors have inadequate locks. Others are so weak they can be levered out of their track. There are some that can be lifted out by hand.

Left Steel windows fit the brickwork.

Far left Plastic (uPVC) windows.
Left Aluminium with a hardwood sub-frame.

Choosing the glass Like most windows, double glazing units are made using 4-mm thick plain glass, though something thicker may be needed if the area to be glazed is large. There are two other options in special cases. The first is patterned or coloured glass – commonly used to provide privacy – which you can have as part of your custom-made sealed unit.

The other option is toughened glass. It is essential for safety where ordinary doors and low-level windows are concerned – anywhere, in fact, where there is a risk of anyone accidentally walking or falling on to the glass.

Style It is important to consider how

Far right Wood frames come in many styles. *Right* Steel with a wood sub-frame.

double glazing will affect the look of your home. Sealed units are barely distinguishable from single glazing, but if they are part of a replacement window, you should choose the window style with care. If your home has a distinct architectural style, choose windows that match the originals.

It is well worth avoiding windows that are totally out of character. You cannot modernize an old house with new windows, nor turn a new house into a period gem with 'period-style' ones!

Where to buy Like many home improvement industries, double glazing has attracted its share of shady dealers. Apart from obvious precautions such as not buying from doorstep salesmen without checking, make sure the company you are dealing with is a member of the Glass and Glazing Federation (6

Mount Row, London W1), or some other established trade organization. If you are still in doubt, check with a local consumer advice centre. They may be able to tell you of firms to avoid in your area.

Having found a reputable company, though, there are still a few points worth bearing in mind. For a start, many of the large firms subcontract their work to local installers, and it is not uncommon for these to be given a fair amount of flexibility when it comes to pricing, so it may be worth enquiring about the possibility of getting a better deal for the job.

You tend to stand more chance of getting one during the spring and summer – the industry's slack period. In fact, these are the best times to order, whether you get a discount or not. Most people think about double glazing during the autumn and winter, but order then and you'll find yourself on a waiting list which will either mean suffering the discomfort of having windows ripped out in the depths of winter, or else not getting your double glazing until some time during the following year.

You can expect to pay upwards of £150 per square metre for replacement windows, so £2,000 to double-glaze a modest home is not an unusual figure. At these prices, it might well be advisable only to double-glaze those windows where the job is most needed, such as in a bathroom for example, and then to double-glaze further rooms if you're pleased with the results.

Curtains, tracks and blinds

Curtains are very much a matter of personal choice, but deciding on the right track or pole involves many practical considerations, too.

Uncorded tracks in plastic or aluminium are one of the cheapest options; many allow the closed curtains to overlap and can be converted to cord operation. There is almost no limit to the length of run, but some (notably those made of plastic) are unsuitable for heavy curtains.

Corded tracks come next in the price scale. Simplest to install are extendable or telescopic tracks, suitable only for straight runs, but ready-corded and neat enough not to need a pelmet. There's a range of standard sizes to cope with runs from 70cm (26in) to as much as 5.5m (18ft).

For a longer, or angled run you need made-to-measure track either with concealed cording or exposed (the latter needs a pelmet). All can be cut to length, bent and corded to meet your precise requirements. In most cases this type of track is best installed by the supplier.

Another option is a curtain pole – a straight rod fitted with a finial at each end and carrying a set of rings to which the curtains are attached. They are for straight runs only and don't allow the curtains to overlap. Corded versions are rare. They may be wood or metal (very often brass).

Blinds Roller blinds in many decorative forms are the most basic, the majority being sold made to measure between 60cm (2ft) and 3m (10ft) wide, with drops between 1m (3ft 3in) and 3m (10ft). You can also purchase kit blinds for cutting to fit.

These blinds are operated by a sprung roller which counterbalances the fabric and should allow you to set the blind at any position.

Venetian blinds have two separate controls – a cord for lifting and a rod or cord for tilting the slats. The slats are either 25, 35 or 50mm (1, 1½ or 2in) wide and usually made of aluminium. Venetian blinds come in widths which range

Opposite Split-cane, 'Austrian' and vertical louvre blinds.

Above Roman blind and (*below*) matching curtain and blind.

Right Fo[...]
ensure [...]
the trac[...]
ceiling [...]
Far righ[...]
are in th[...]
nail tim[...]
between[...]
into the[...]

betw
with
Ve
89 o
weig
over
rota
ious
(per
alun

As
louv
widt
up t

In
blin
facti
whic
blin
and
thre
cor
clea

Inst

Hav
blin
will

M
esp
dow
heig
mid
dim
sate
a bi

If
win
little
rev

C
thai
clea
dra

F
abo
wal
upp
Thi
allo
effi

H
cre
this
dri
doi

16.
ADDING ON: LOFT CONVERSIONS

Making use of the generous amount of space available in the lofts of many homes is easily the most economic and convenient method of increasing the size of the house. And with the costs – and complications – of moving home being what they are today, a loft conversion is a very attractive proposition if you're simply looking for more room.

Above A comfortable work area created inside a modest roof space. *Right* From the outside – the new dormer window blends easily with the existing exterior.

There are numerous purposes to which you can put your loft. It could simply be a storage area – somewhere to keep oddments that might otherwise cause clutter in bedrooms or other rooms. Alternatively, it could be a store for garden furniture in winter, or out-of-season sports gear.

For these uses, a conversion need only be of the simplest type. You might fix a few floorboards to the joists to provide somewhere secure to stand when you haul yourself up through the trap door, and you should certainly fit a loft ladder. This is a very much safer means of access than an ordinary pair of steps.

If you want to create proper living quarters – in the jargon of the planning officer a 'habitable room' – then your conversion must comply with the appropriate requirements of the Building Regulations.

The joists will have to be strengthened so that they can take the weight of a new floor, because the existing ones are probably capable of supporting only a

ceiling. Walls, a doorway and ceiling will have to be added. You will need windows to give enough light and ventilation and there must be sufficient headroom. And you will need a proper fixed stairway.

To do all this you will require specialist help. You will certainly need a builder, and you should use the services either of an architect or a building surveyor to draw up working plans for the job and supervise the builder. Or you can opt for the all-in service offered by a number of loft-conversion specialists who operate on a national basis. Converting a loft is not a do-it-yourself job, although you can certainly undertake certain finishing tasks and, of course, the decoration, yourself.

The most obvious purpose for a loft conversion is to provide extra bedrooms. If you allocate these to the children, they can spend their free time that much further away from the distractions of downstairs – usually a mutually agreeable arrangement!

Alternatively, the conversion could be used as a general hobby room for all the family. But it's not a good place for a games room: the noise from table tennis, for example, would reverberate around the whole house.

If you live in an area of particular natural beauty, a living room in the loft might allow you to take maximum advantage of the views. Bear in mind, though, that a long climb up several flights of stairs might have diminishing appeal to older members of the family. This is an important point to remember if you're considering using a loft as a 'granny flat'.

The rooms least suitable for the loft are those that require a water supply. British plumbing works on the basis of water pumped by mains pressure to a cold storage tank in the loft. This feeds most of the house – cold taps, WCs, hot water system – by gravity. The higher the tank is above the point at which you need the water, the greater the pressure of the supply. So there will be insufficient pressure for a loft bathroom unless you either raise the cold tank very high in the roof space or else install a pumped system.

Access Loft ladders that retract into the loft space are fine if the space is merely for storage, but if the room is to be frequently used you need a proper staircase. You can choose either a conventional type or a spiral, so long as the one you opt for complies with the Building Regulations. Try to ensure that the new staircase is in a style in keeping with that of your home and bear in mind that spiral staircases can present practical difficulties – not least when it comes to moving furniture.

Finding room for a new staircase is possible by modifying the existing stairwell or perhaps encroaching on a boxroom. However, the latter cancels out the gain in living space which, after all, is the aim of the conversion. In any event, the stair position you choose must allow at least 2m (6ft 7in) of headroom above the entire flight, including the landing at the top.

Fire safety There are four basic rules to follow if you are to comply with the relevant regulations.

The main stairwell, the new landing/ stairway into the loft, plus any route between the two, should be separated from the rest of the house by walls capable of resisting a fire for 30 minutes or one hour (depending on how many storeys there are in the house). Therefore it is unlikely that you will be able to undertake a conversion if your house has an open-plan design.

In most cases, this fire-resistant shaft containing the stairway must lead directly to an external door through which, in an emergency, you can leave the building and escape to safety.

Doors leading into the fire-resistant shaft must also offer adequate fire resistance (which means existing ones may have to be modified or replaced) and they must be fitted with automatic door closers (rising butt hinges will not do).

Finally, it may be necessary to upgrade the fire resistance of the floors in all upper storeys. This is usually done by covering the floorboards with hardboard sheets.

In addition, although not specifically required by the regulations, if the loft is to be turned into a bedroom, it is well worth equipping the stairwell with smoke detector alarms.

Insulation in the loft is absolutely vital, otherwise the room will be icy cold in winter and roasting in summer. So the walls and ceiling must be insulated with glass fibre blanket or with polystyrene board at least 100mm (4in) thick.

The insulation work should be carried out before the new walls and ceiling are put up. It should be possible to fit blanket or board between the rafters without the need for battens to hold the material in place. A polythene vapour barrier should be stapled over the insulation to minimize condensation.

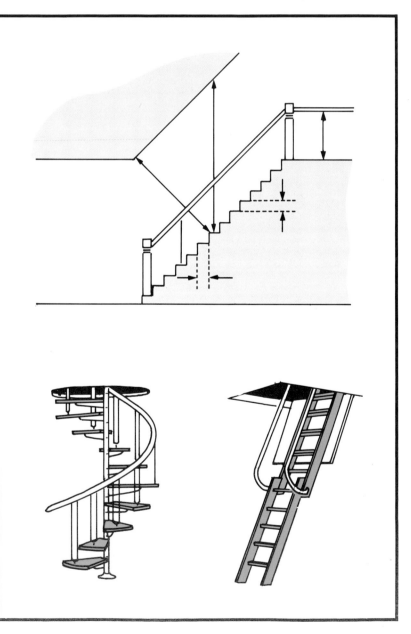

Below Your choice of stairway must conform to regulations covering headroom, handrails and fire safety.

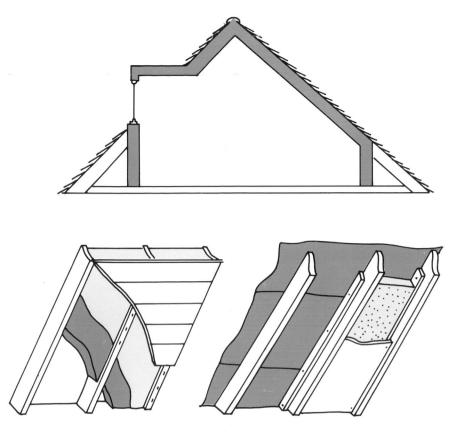

There are two places to fit windows: in the end wall of a dormer, or as roof-lights. The latter are much cheaper provided you can get the necessary height.

Choose your loft windows with great care: unless they match your existing ones, the extension will not blend into your home's overall exterior appearance.

A dormer is effectively the key to most loft conversion, since it allows you to break out of the awkward, pitched shape and create a larger room. More-over, a dormer helps you to conform with the headroom requirements of the Building Regulations. There are three basic types of dormer: through, single and bay. The bay reaches to the outside wall of the house, and can incorporate picture windows or, if you are over-looked, waist-high windows with an infill panel below.

Above All walls and ceilings must be insulated. Blanket or board fitted between rafters should be covered with a vapour barrier before cladding is put up. Where rafters are to be left exposed, insulate between and fit plasterboard on top – this can be decorated later.

Windows form an integral part of your loft room because they supply not just light but the ventilation required under the Building Regulations, which state that the opening parts of the window, together with any air bricks, should amount to at least one-twentieth of the total area of the room measured at any imaginary horizontal plane 1.5m (4ft 11in) above the floor.

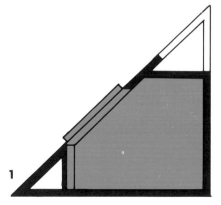

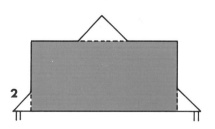

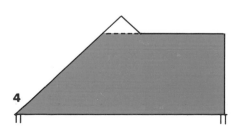

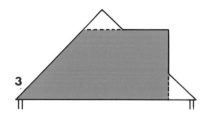

Right Your choice of windows includes **1** roof-lights, **2** a through dormer, **3** a single dormer, **4** a bay dormer, and **5** a single (or through) dormer with balcony.

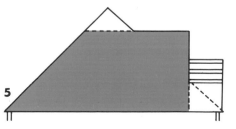

17.
ADDING ON: EXTENSIONS

An extension can be anything from a ready-made porch to an additional storey. But however modest or grand, any such enlargement of your home deserves to be considered in relation to the overall structure – because to be a success, every extension should look as if it's been an integral part of the house from the beginning.

Building an extension is the most radical improvement you can make to a house, so it's a project that deserves careful planning. The first matters to resolve are threefold. What is the extension required for? How large is it going to be? Where will it be?

Limitations of land, money and the existing shape of your home will make all these questions simpler to answer, of course, but it is nevertheless vital to know exactly what you are looking for before you call in an architect or surveyor to draw up plans.

Remember that if you want an extension to create, say, a much larger kitchen that will accommodate an eating area, this may leave you with a dining room for which there is no longer an immediate purpose. Consequently, you may end up rearranging the whole ground floor of your house. In other words, think of an extension not just in terms of an extra bit of space, but as something that might allow you to replan your home as a whole.

As far as size is concerned, the architect's estimate for construction costs will be the twin restricting factor to the simple limitations imposed by the land available (as well as the confines of planning permission, about which more later). Remember that you can build up

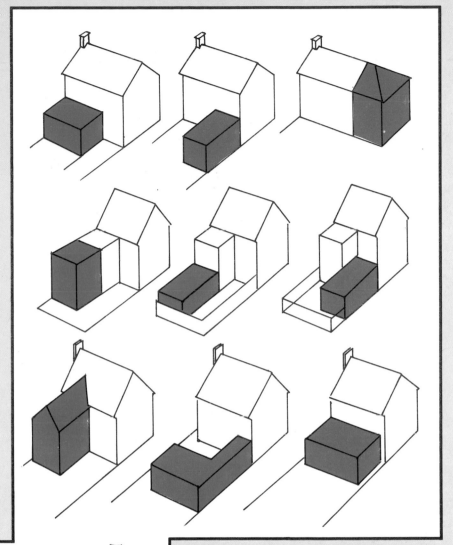

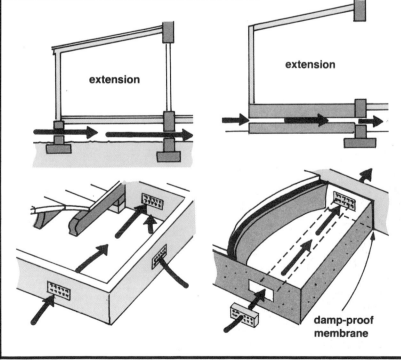

as well as out – and that a two-storey extension built as one project is likely to be very much more economic than building each floor at separate stages.

As to where you can build, this is partly governed by the shape of your house, by the closeness of neighbours and also by your house's aspect. As the drawings (opposite) show, shadows play an important part in planning – because the last thing you want an extension to do is to overshadow your house for the greater part of the day. Similarly, it's worthwhile trying to avoid building an extension that is itself overshadowed by the existing house or by adjacent buildings.

For all the restrictions, however, there are still a number of extension options open to most home owners – as the assortment of ideas sketched on these pages illustrates.

Left Nearing completion – the reward for the planning work that has gone before.

Planning regulations, you should note, differ, depending on the function of the new structure, so it is important to know what your requirements are. Single-storey buildings, for example, fall into two categories: (1) with solid walls and ceiling for full-time habitation; and (2) with all-round glass and a ceiling lower than 2.3m (7ft 7in) for use as a sun room.

The rules and restrictions

You may not be allowed to do exactly what you want because of certain restrictions affecting your property. So always check first – usually with your local authority – to see if any of the following apply to you.

Restrictive covenants on the title deeds or land registration certificates of the property. Have a look at the documents, which are usually held by the mortgagee or building society that advanced the money to buy the house.

Conditional planning consent Sometimes planning permission to build housing estates, or even an individual building, may have been granted only with the proviso that certain conditions are adhered to. These conditions may prevent you from building any kind of extension, so be sure to check with the local authority.

Listed buildings If you live in one, *any* proposed work requires consent.

Designated conservation areas If you live in one, you face virtually the same limitations as those applying to listed buildings.

Tree preservation orders may apply to any number of trees in your garden, preventing you chopping them down to make way for new building.

Ground lease If your home is not freehold, your ground lease will probably contain covenants controlling the kind of work you are allowed to do. You will need the landlord's consent.

If you are planning *any* structural changes to your home, you must notify the planning department of your local authority. They will ask for detailed specifications of the proposed work, including the planned method of construction and the materials to be used. Depending on what you are building, you may have to seek planning permission first.

Many home improvements need no planning permission, but all have to comply with the Building Regulations.

Under your mortgage terms the mortgagee (building society or bank) is entitled to be consulted about any structural alterations and to inspect the building regulations consent. If you are applying for a loan or for a second mortgage you will need to supply a set of building regulations plans with your application.

Neighbours Ask them for their views *before* you seek local authority permission. The local council will probably write to them anyway to ask them if they

Permission is *not* required if the extension is under 70 cubic metres (2500cu ft) or 15 per cent of the existing volume of the house up to 115 cubic metres (4600cu ft) or whichever is the greater. (This does not apply to terraced properties.)

have any objections, once you have made your formal submission.

Planning permission is required on certain types of work only and is intended to protect neighbours from a potential eyesore. Where permission is required the local authority will vet all drawings.

Permission *is* required if the extension proposed will be higher than the original roof, or if it will project beyond the building's nearest point to the highway – the building line – or dangerously obscure road users' view, or block sunlight from a neighbour's windows. Applications are also required for extensions above gound-floor level within 2m (6ft 7in) of site boundaries, or where the development covers more than half the area of a garden.

Above
1 Boundary walls and fences under 2m need no planning permission.
2 A swimming pool covering more than half the garden needs consent. **3** Planning permission would be needed for this substantial extension because it projects beyond the building line.
4 The garage is under 3m high and meets other requirements, so no permission is needed.
5 Fences and walls fronting the highway can be no higher than 1m without permission. **6** Oil storage tanks up to 770 gallons do not need consent but must be no higher than 3m. **7** Trees subject to preservation order cannot be felled for extension building.
8 Hedges are not affected by planning control.

Right A vertical extension that raises the building height requires planning consent. A loft conversion with dormers that do not raise the height of the building would not normally require permission.

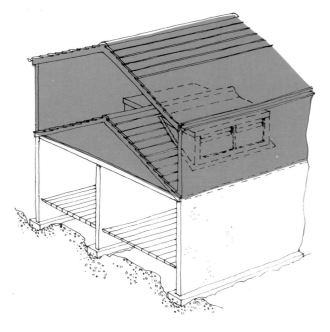

Garden sheds, greenhouses, summer houses and small swimming pools do not normally require planning permission, provided they meet the following requirements:

Any pitched roof building must not exceed 4m (13ft) in height. Flat roof structures must not exceed 3m (10ft). The structure must not extend beyond the front of the main dwelling nor cover more than half the garden area and it should not require either a new access from the public road or alteration to the existing one.

Storage tanks for central heating oil require planning permission if they hold more than 3500 litres (770 gallons), are more than 3m (10ft) above ground, or project beyond the building line.

Any fence that adjoins the highway and is not more than 1m (39in) high – or 2m (6ft 7in) elsewhere – and does not obstruct road users' field of vision does not require planning permission. Hedges are not affected by planning regulations.

Applying If you have not yet finalized the details of your extension you can make a preliminary application for outline planning permission. You just need to provide the bare details of your scheme and, provided you have the council's agreement, you do not have to submit a detailed plan. If outline permission is granted, you will still have to submit full details for approval later, but you will of course have minimized your risk of rejection at that stage.

If you are considering buying a property to which you would like to add an

Below Unlikely to be granted planning consent, this extension conflicts in style with the house and blocks light from the house next door.

extension, you are entitled to apply for planning consent before the building is legally yours.

Where planning permission is required there will be numerous forms to fill in. These forms, together with guidance on the information you will have to submit for approval, are available at the planning office of your local council. Depending on your council's administrative requirements, you may have to submit up to four copies of the appropriate plans. These do not have to be drawn up by a professional. If you feel competent you can do them yourself,

A *key plan* (scale of not less than 1:2500) may be needed if the block plan is not sufficiently clear.

Where any work subject to building regulations is carried out a local authority surveyor will inspect the site when work starts and then again at intervals until completion to ensure that the regulations are observed. You will have to pay the council a modest fee related to the value of the work.

Specialist help Unless you are a very competent do-it-yourselfer you will need professional services to design

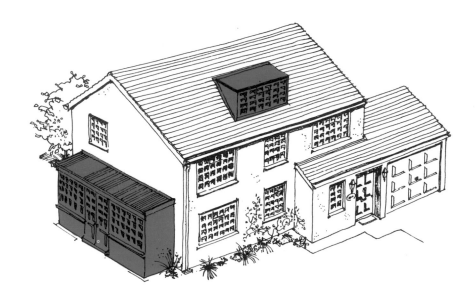

Right You can build a conservatory or sun lounge or enclose a veranda without planning permission if the size of the structure is no more than 15% of the volume of the house.

but make sure they are clear and legible and give all the required information.

The council will advise you of just what information is needed, and this will include details of the materials you propose to use as well as comprehensive information about proposed drains, water supply and heating.

Depending on the type of work planned, up to three separate types of drawing may have to be submitted:

A *block plan* (scale of not less than 1:1250) to show the extension's position in relation to the existing building, the boundaries and adjoining streets and properties.

Building plans (scale of not less than 1:100) to provide the necessary construction details.

and build your extension. For smaller home improvements a chartered building surveyor should be able to help you, and where the design of the finished structure is important a chartered architect may well be needed. Discuss your plans with likely candidates and ask them for their opinions; you should soon find one who is on your wavelength. Make sure that you don't forget to ask for an estimate of the architect's fees.

The architect may recommend a number of builders, but you may prefer to use a firm that has been recommended to you by a friend or neighbour – usually the most reliable method of choosing, especially if you get the opportunity to inspect work already done by the builder in question.

Porches

Completely open porches (the types which are fitted as standard to many homes) do little more than keep callers dry while they wait at the door. It's only the totally enclosed porch that can make a really useful contribution to your home.

To begin with, an enclosed porch can provide some useful storage space – not just for boots and umbrellas but perhaps for a pram or bicycle. It makes an ideal dropping-off place for deliveries and, in the case of a glass porch, can also function as an attractive small greenhouse.

Whatever size and type of porch you finally choose, perhaps the most practical benefit of an enclosed one is that it makes your house warmer. It does this partly by acting as a sort of airlock, preventing the blast of cold air you would otherwise receive every time you open the front door, and partly by eliminating most of the chilly draughts.

It would be a mistake, though, to imagine that these energy savings meant that the porch pays for itself. The real benefit will be in terms of comfort, because a cold hall can make an entire house seem chilly. And an open-plan home or one in which the front door opens directly on to the living area will benefit particularly from a porch in this respect.

Choosing the type and style Probably the simplest way to build a porch is with a kit. They are available in timber or aluminium, and are designed either to fill in an existing open porch or to be built as a complete unit from scratch. Softwood models are the cheapest, but need regular painting if they are to last. Aluminium, cedar and hardwood versions should look after themselves (though wood ones will require regular varnishing), but they will be more expensive.

Kit manufacturers will usually give you advice on the most suitable type of porch, on overcoming any design problems and on obtaining any local authority approval that you may find to be necessary. They will supply every-

A porch should look as if
it has been part of the
house all along.

thing you require to build the porch
itself – including the glass – except for
the base. All you have to do is follow
their instructions and put the whole
thing together.

With the exception of a few
'Georgian-style' designs, most kits
have the simple, sparse look of a greenhouse. So as far as looks are concerned,
this type of porch is best suited to fairly
modern houses.

Some manufacturers will design
porches individually to your needs but,
in practice, the results don't look very
different from the standard kits, and you
would do well to think of them as variations on the basic theme.

For an entirely custom-made porch
designed specifically for your style of
home you can either construct it yourself or call in a builder.

For enthusiastic do-it-yourselfers
with experience in construction work a
porch need present no problems, but
for most of us the option of calling in a

professional would be the wiser move. After all, a porch is about the most conspicuous extension you can make to your home – it's a job that needs doing well.

A chartered surveyor or a reputable builder who can offer a design service would be well worth considering for this sort of job. If the work calls for a certain amount of artistic flair – for example, if you have a very old house with a distinctive character – you should think about using an architect.

Rules and restrictions In most cases, provided you do not share the house with another family, you can build a porch without planning permission. But there are a number of conditions to be met: the porch must have a total floor area of less than 2sq m (21sq ft); it must be less than 3m (10ft) high; and no part of it may come within 2m (6ft 7in) of a public footpath or road.

That having been said, however, the planning regulations can be complicated by the fact that one local authority's interpretation of them might vary from that of another. So always check before you start. If the council say planning permission is not required, get it in writing just to be sure.

Whether or not you need planning permission, you will certainly need Building Regulations Approval from the council's Building Controls Officer before you can begin. He will want to know – as is the case with all structural work – whether the materials and methods you are planning to use conform with the regulations.

It's highly unlikely that you will have problems if you are buying a kit, or having the porch designed and built for you. If you do, refer any queries from the council to the people supplying the porch and let them sort it out.

You may, however, have a few difficulties if you are designing the porch yourself. The best thing to do is take your plans along to the Building Control Officer as early as possible and discuss them with him. He won't redesign the porch for you, but he may make some valuable suggestions.

His main concern will be that the porch is structurally sound, and that it in no way weakens the existing building. He will also have to be satisfied that, if the porch base is higher than the house damp proof course, you will alter the damp proof course level of the house accordingly.

Drainage is also covered by the regulations. You must make adequate arrangements to carry rainwater away from the porch, either into a rain barrel, or into a soakaway pit somewhere in the garden. And if the porch is over a manhole, the manhole cover (which must still be accessible) will have to be replaced with one that is both airtight and watertight. In certain cases you may be required to provide a double cover.

Finally, if the porch is within 1m (3ft 3in) of the boundary with a neighbouring property, it must offer a reasonable degree of resistance to fire. The building regulations in this instance can be somewhat complicated, so check with the council that your proposals won't bring you into conflict with these important rules.

Safety Whichever kind of porch you choose, do make sure that it is safe and secure.

Avoid creating awkward steps that could cause the unwary to trip, or that might make it difficult to haul a pram or a wheeled shopping basket over. Leave plenty of room for doors to open. If you are installing a porch that is composed largely of glass, make quite certain that you use regulation safety glass, at least at lower levels – and throughout if there is likely to be any risk that someone might accidentally collide with the panes.

Remember, too, that a porch provides the perfect cover for a burglar to get to work on your front door. This is particularly true of a porch with patterned glass or one that is not lit at night. So you are strongly advised to keep both your front door and your porch door securely locked.

You should also lock any windows of the house that can be reached from the roof of the porch, because it probably won't be all that difficult for a burglar to climb on to it. A useful deterrent in this

It's very important that a porch should be designed to fit in with the style and period of the building.

case is to use special non-drying paint on the new downpipe for the guttering. At the very least, you should fit a light in the porch, and if possible, an external light as well.

Finally, bear in mind that the 'greenhouse effect' of your porch can make it extremely hot in bright sunshine. And if you don't want to invite burglars by leaving the porch door open for half the summer, be sure to install opening windows so that you can ventilate the porch without the need to take undesirable security risks.

18.
OUTSIDE VIEW: PAVING

Paths and driveways are worked hard in most homes, and therefore need regular attention – and occasional replacement. For good looks and a long-lasting surface, paving is ideal, provided you use appropriate materials and make a thorough job of the preparation work.

Planning a path

This is very largely a matter of finding an arrangement that is both practical and good looking.

At the front of the house, for example, to eliminate potential short cuts through flower beds or across grass, lay the path in a straight line between the front door and the garden gate. If this is not feasible, consider moving the garden gate to create a better route.

It is obviously not in the interest of safety to use materials that get slippery when wet. However, incorporating steps is a more serious hazard. As a rule, the easier steps are to use, the safer they are, so avoid making them either too high or too low: 100mm to 200mm (4in to 8in) is recommended. A common error is to have steps so near a gate that there is no room for the gate to open and close with you standing there.

Finally, avoid turning a sloping path into a continuous flight of steps. On a long, steep slope especially, that is asking for trouble. Break the flight into manageable sections with a fair-sized 'landing' between each.

Designing a drive

As with paths, a drive is normally best laid along the most direct route to the garage. Do make sure that it will be long enough to take the car and still leave room for gates and garage doors to

open and that there's space either side to get in and out of the car. Don't line the drive with shrubs or trees – not only because they can be a nuisance when you're getting in or out of the car but also because overhanging trees may shed branches, leaves, blossom and sap on to the car.

If you are thinking of building a new drive where one does not already exist, you will almost certainly need planning permission – the exception is on private roads, but even then it is best to check. You must be able to show that you can come and go in safety. Basically, that means ensuring that you can see clearly

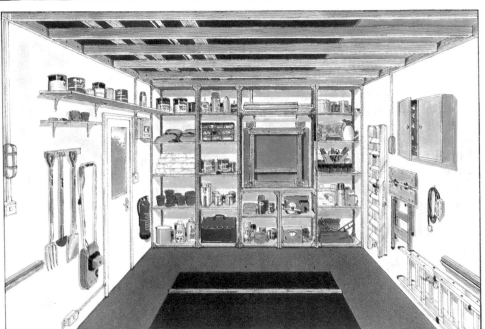

19.
OUTSIDE VIEW:
THE GARAGE

A garage can – and should – be an invaluable storage and work place for all sorts of items and functions as well as the car and all that goes with it. By improving the use to which you put your garage you can take much of the strain off overloaded parts of your home, and make all sorts of DIY jobs much more practical and pleasurable into the bargain.

A garage can be more or less anything you want it to be, from simply somewhere to keep the car to a fully equipped utility room. Whatever your choice, all garages have a few basic requirements. You will need storage space and a power supply to run tools and machinery and to provide heating and lighting. You may need a water supply and drainage. And consider security. Even if the contents of your garage don't seem worth stealing, the tools you keep there might be used by a burglar to break into your home.

General repairs Garages can be treated like any other building. Regular maintenance is necessary to prevent serious defects, including making sure that the roof is weatherproof and undertaking regular decoration. Also, woodwork needs painting to protect it from the weather, while the interior walls will benefit from a coat of white paint to reflect light, making working conditions better.

You might also consider enlarging the garage. If it was originally made from a kit this is usually straightforward, unless it has a pent roof – in which case you can extend only lengthways.

Garage doors Replacing old doors is another worthwhile improvement and

modern up-and-over doors – those that retract beneath the garage roof – are far more convenient than side-hinged doors.

There are two main types. One uses a cantilever action: springs in the door frame counterbalance the door and pull it into the open position when released. The second type is more robust, and more expensive: spring counterweights carry the open door right into the garage along overhead tracks which are capable of coping with the heaviest of doors.

Both types come in a variety of styles. Most are ribbed steel or aluminium, giving a sort of slatted effect, or are moulded in glass fibre to produce panelled period-style doors – usually Georgian. There are sizes to suit most modern garages, but you may have a certain amount of difficulty finding one to fit an older building. Some firms will modify standard door sizes to suit, or will alter the size of the door opening by adding a substantial timber subframe.

Finally, consider fitting the new door with an automatic opener. This is especially useful on large, heavy doors, but also offers worthwhile benefits with doors of any size. For one thing, it improves your garage's security. For another it overcomes the problem of the

Left Garage doors can be architecturally acceptable as well as purely practical.

flames – garages are a potential fire risk at the best of times. A wall-mounted electric fan heater is a much better bet and should not get in your way while you are working.

Good ventilation is necessary to avoid a build-up of fumes. When working on the car with the engine running you should always have ventilation, so an open window or powered extractor fan will be necessary if you don't have the garage door open.

Keep within reach a fire extinguisher of a type that is handy and safe for use on electrical and petrol fires. A blanket extinguisher is a good idea for smothering small fires caused by petrol or oil spills.

Adding a garage

If you're planning a new garage, first decide whether it is to be joined to the house. A connected garage is certainly more convenient and offers greater possibilities for multiple use and improvement. But it is likely to cost more and, to comply with building regulations, it has to be rather more substantially built.

You should think about how you will get the car in and out; in other words, how to position the drive. If getting on and off the road involves crossing a public footpath, you will have to pay the council to put in a ramp. The council will also have to be satisfied that you can come and go without presenting a hazard to other road users.

Custom-built or kit? Garages from kits are widely available and sufficiently varied to meet most needs. They have the advantage of being relatively cheap and easy to put up. If you are reasonably handy, you should be able to tackle the work yourself, given a few able-bodied helpers. Basically, you just put down a concrete base and slot the garage together on top of it. If you prefer to have a kit put up professionally, most local builders should be willing to take the work on.

The drawback of kits is that you may have difficulty getting a good architectural match with your house. Most kit garages have a rather slab-like appearance and, though they come in a variety of finishes (plain concrete, rough pebbledash-style aggregate and even imitation brick and stone), they do not really match the genuine article. In general kit garages are fine if sited well away from the house. If not, you ought to visit a show site to form your own opinion, but for best results be prepared to have the garage custom built.

Custom-built garages are by far the best bet if you want the garage attached to the house. You can then achieve an aesthetic blend of old and new, and you can also design the garage and its foundation so you can add a room extension on top of it at some later date.

Rules and restrictions In theory, unless your garage is particularly large, you should not need planning permission. In practice, you almost certainly will, either because the garage extends beyond the part of your house nearest to a public highway or because it involves creating a new access to a public highway.

Even if you think these conditions do not apply, it is best to check. Your application is unlikely to be refused – most councils are anxious to get parked cars off the roads – unless you live in a conservation area or a listed building or are unable to meet the safety criteria.

In addition, you will require Building Regulations approval. The structural aspects of the Building Regulations are unlikely to present difficulties, however. If they do, get your builder or garage manufacturer to sort them out. The regulations governing fire safety are a little more complicated and it is worth seeking expert advice, particularly if the garage is going to be either close to the boundary of your property or is to be built on to the side of the house.

Last but not least, think about access to the garage. In most cases, your work area will be at one end, allowing you to work even when the car is garaged, so it may be worth having an extra door at the working end to save you having to squeeze past the car. If the garage is to be built on to the side of the house, it is well worth installing a connecting door as part of the job. This will be invaluable when it is pouring with rain.

Right The workings of an up-and-over garage door of the cantilevered type.
Far right A typical track system for an up-and-over door.

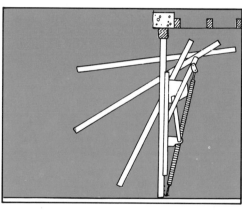

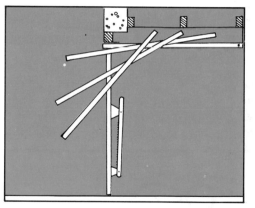

Hedges

A good hedge makes a solid and attractive boundary or screen which will last for many years. The only maintenance required is pruning or clipping to keep it in shape – a job which is made considerably easier with electric trimmers. Choose from evergreens such as holly, yew, laurel and viburnum or flowering varieties such as berberis, rose or pyracantha. Deciduous hedges include beech, hornbeam, hazel and hawthorn.

Planting Mark out the run of the hedge, making sure it will not be too close to a fence or pavement. The soil must be cleared of weeds and a trench dug to a spade's depth, placing the soil to one side. Loosen the soil in the trench for another spade's depth and fork in two buckets of compost per metre. Fill in the topsoil, mixing in two buckets of sphagnum moss peat and 50g (2oz) bonemeal per metre.

Mark out the position for each plant and plant to the depth of the soil mark on the stem. Firm the plant in by treading the soil round it. Water the plants and add a layer of mulch.

Pruning Shaping a hedge from the beginning is important to encourage growth. As soon as the plants are established and beginning to grow, trim back the new shoots by half their length about three or four times a year until the base is dense. As it grows, train the hedge into a wedge shape, with a broad base tapering up to a narrow top, which can be flat or rounded, as you prefer. This allows plenty of light to come in and makes the hedge strong – enabling it both to resist wind and to withstand the weight of snow, which could easily break a broad-topped hedge.

1 When planting, mark out the trench with the plants' mature size in mind. **2** Trim the growing hedge into a wedge shape for stability. **3** A tight, rounded top sheds snow more efficiently. **4** Don't shape your hedge this way: a base as wide as the hedge is tall takes up too much space and is difficult to trim. **5** A badly shaped hedge: all the growth is at the top, and the base sparse and untidy. The top is unstable and can easily be damaged by wind and snow.

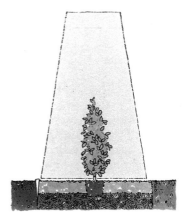

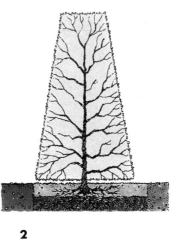

1

2

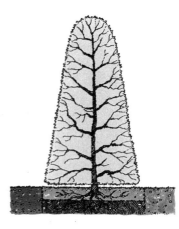

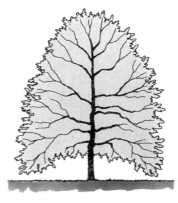

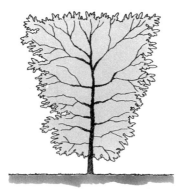

3

4

5

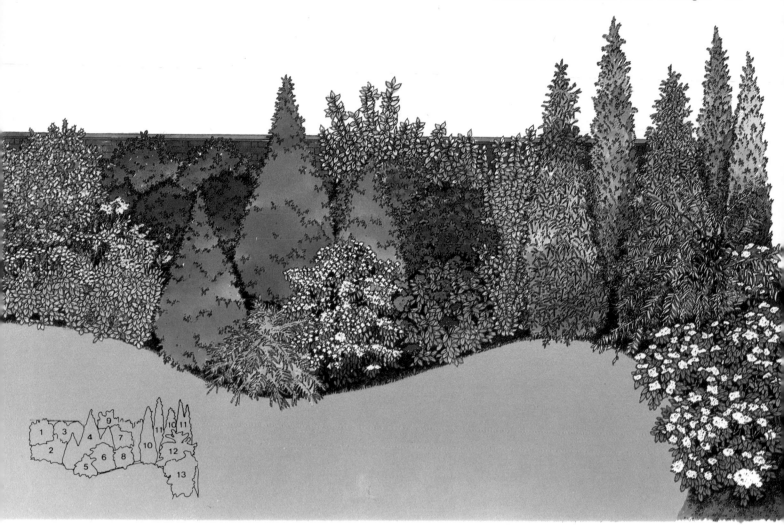

A screen of densely leaved evergreens is an effective and year-round source of privacy, and can even reduce noise levels if planted along your garden's boundary with, say, a busy road. In this planting plan, flowering deciduous shrubs are mixed in to provide colour and interest.

1 Ilex aquifolium 'Madame Briot', Golden Variegated Holly. Easily grown evergreen shrub with spiny, leathery leaves. Grows to between 4.5m (15ft) and 9m (30ft) but can be trimmed.

2 Senecio greyi. Evergreen shrub with dense, broad mounds of grey, felt-like foliage. Reaches 1m (3¼ft) high and 2m (6½ft) wide.

3 Berberis thunbergii atropurpurea. Deciduous shrub with dark, plum-coloured foliage. Up to 1.5m (5ft) high.

4 Thuya plicata, Western Red Cedar. Evergreen conifer reaching 18m (60ft) high.

5 Juniperus × media 'Tsitzerana Aurea', Juniper. Conifer spreading 2m (6½ft) or more and 1m (3¼ft) high. Gold-yellow foliage.

6 Viburnum plicatum 'Lanarth', Japanese Snowball. Deciduous shrub reaching 3m (10ft) high. Easy to grow.

7 Cotinus coggyria 'Royal Purple', Smoke Tree. Deciduous shrub reaching 2.5m (8ft) to 4m (13ft), with smooth, rounded, deep purple leaves and pink-grey flowers.

8 Spiraea × bumalda 'Anthony Waterer'. Dwarf deciduous shrub forming compact mounds 30cm (1ft) to 60cm (2ft) high.

9 Cornus alba 'Elegantissima', Dogwood. Deciduous shrub grown for its attractive red stems which form a thicket up to 3m (10ft) high with cream and white leaves.

10 Chamaecyparis lawsoniana 'Stewartii', Lawson Cypress. Conifer, slowly growing to between 10m (35ft) and 18m (60ft).

11 Chamaecyparis lawsoniana 'Columnaris Glauca', Lawson Cypress. A faster-growing variety of the above with dark blue-green foliage.

12 Cotoneaster salicifolius. Semi-deciduous shrub reaching 3m (10ft) high. Arching branches covered with long, pointed leaves.

13 Viburnum tinus. Evergreen shrub reaching 3m (10ft) high; small, dark green glossy leaves and pinky-white flowers throughout winter.

No matter what you choose to mark a boundary, you can be reasonably sure that it will be expensive. It makes sense to think carefully about what you need. For example, if all you want is a way to mark a boundary, there is little point in going to the expense of having a really high fence. And as low fences by their very nature can be peered over, it would be a waste of money to get one that's expensively made so it can't be peered through!

Of course, there are practical matters to be taken into account as well and the main one is probably durability. As a general rule, you may expect to get what you pay for. So a cheap, softwood fence can hardly be expected to last anything like as long as an expensive brick wall. All the same, making a good job of erecting a fence and maintaining it afterwards should add years to its useful life.

Types of fencing The traditional peep-proof fence is closeboard, which is made from stout planks nailed to horizontal rails between posts. The waney-edged boards make overlap fencing look similar to rustic horizontal closeboard, but the wood is thinner and needs framing for additional strength. Probably the cheapest way in which to maintain your privacy is to put up interwoven fencing. Alternatively, you might try chain link, although this is not by any means the most attractive choice and is best screened with plants.

Picket or palisade fencing usually tends to be cheaper than other wooden fences, but it affords little privacy. There are several decorative styles to choose from. Chestnut paling is just about as cheap a fence as you will find – simply a collection of stakes strung together with wire.

You may think of trellis as being rather flimsy but robust types are available and, with climbing plants, they can make excellent and economic screens. Another low-cost idea is traditional ranch – or post and rail – fencing, which you can build yourself using sawn planks or rustic half logs. You can make it as high or as low as you like and you can even make it peep-proof by fixing

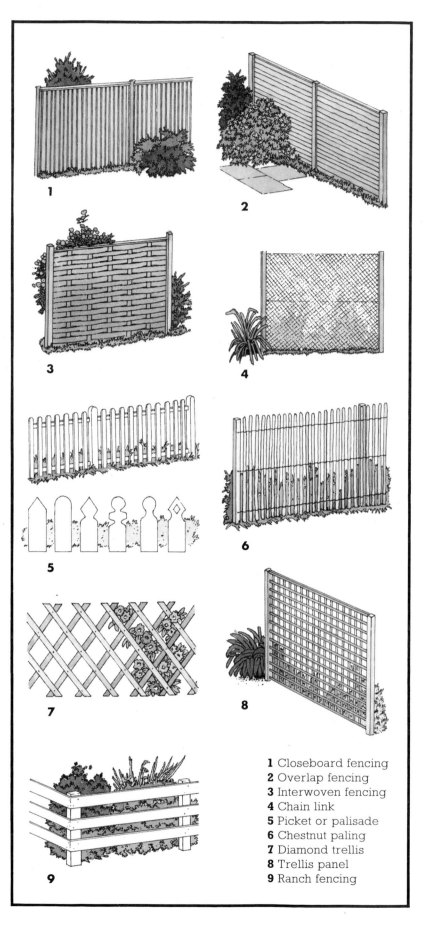

1 Closeboard fencing
2 Overlap fencing
3 Interwoven fencing
4 Chain link
5 Picket or palisade
6 Chestnut paling
7 Diamond trellis
8 Trellis panel
9 Ranch fencing

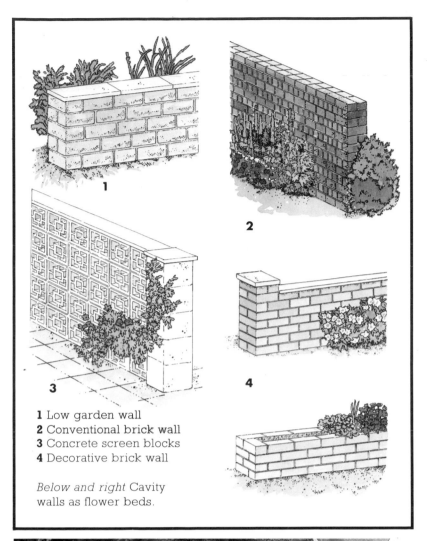

1 Low garden wall
2 Conventional brick wall
3 Concrete screen blocks
4 Decorative brick wall

Below and right Cavity
walls as flower beds.

planks alternately to either side of the posts.

Types of wall Brick is the obvious choice. There's a wide range of colours and textures to choose from for making walls of any height or decorative appearance. As an alternative to brick you can buy many different designs of concrete screen blocks to make very attractive walls.

While these materials are very hardwearing, it is best to use special-quality materials where there is constant exposure to the elements – particularly on the tops of walls. Remember, however, that low-cavity walls can also double as miniature flower beds.

Legal aspects The law relating to hedges, fences and walls is a complicated tangle of new, old and ancient legislation.

Don't go by post positions. The only way to tell who owns a fence is to look at the property deeds – and even they may not tell you. What's more, there is no guarantee that any barrier marks the actual boundary.

Unless there is something in the deeds to the contrary (which is quite likely on new housing estates), you don't have to put up fences at all. Nor are you obliged to maintain them (though beware if they are a nuisance or encroach on your neighbour's land), which is just as well, since the need to repair a fence doesn't give you the legal right to trespass.

Virtually the only part of the law concerning fencing that is reasonably straightforward is the Planning Regulations. You need permission to build a fence or wall higher than two metres (6ft 7in) or one metre (3ft 3in) if the boundary faces a highway. Hedges are free from control.

Where does that leave you in the event of a dispute with neighbours? Although it's easier said than done, you should try to find a compromise if this is at all possible. Legal action is never cheap and, once having gone to court, you will probably have to accept a compromise in any case.

INDEX